D1080097

Potatoes

Potatoes

p

This is a Parragon Book
First published in 2000

Parragon
Queen Street House
4 Queen Street
Bath BA1 1HE, UK

ISBN: 0-75254-885-9

Printed in Indonesia

NOTE

This book uses metric and imperial measurements. Follow the same units of measurement throughout; do not mix metric and imperial.
All spoon measurements are level: teaspoons are assumed to be 5 ml, and tablespoons are assumed to be 15 ml. Unless otherwise stated,
milk is assumed to be full fat, eggs and individual vegetables such as potatoes are medium,
and pepper is freshly ground black pepper.

Recipes using raw or very lightly cooked eggs should be
avoided by infants, the elderly, pregnant women, convalescents, and anyone
suffering from an illness.

Contents

Introduction 8 Regional Cooking 10–13
Using Potatoes 14 How to Use This Book 16

Soups, Starters & Salads

Light Meals & Side Dishes

Light Meals & Side Dishes

(continued)

Vegetarian/ Vegan Suppers

Vegetable Savouries

Fish Dishes

Poultry & Meat

Bread & Desserts

Introduction

Easy to grow and cook, inexpensive, wonderfully tasty, extremely nutritious and highly versatile, it is not surprising that the potato is one of the world's most popular vegetables and an important staple food, which is cultivated almost everywhere.

There is a vast range of different varieties of potato – around 3,000 in all – although only about 100 of these are regularly grown. Each variety has its own distinctive shape, texture and colour, and reflects the country to which it is native, from the firm yellow flesh of the Jersey Royal new potato to the rich, warm orange of the yam from the Caribbean.

Possibly dating from as far back as 3000 BCE, the potato originated in South America, where it was known as the 'papa'. It was eaten by the Incas, fresh when it was in season and dried in winter. Its existence was not brought to the attention of the rest of the world until the 16th century, however, when Peru fell to the Spanish conquistador Francisco Pizarro. Peru was well known to be rich in minerals, and it was the mineral traders who began to introduce the potato elsewhere.

In Europe, the potato arrived via Spain, and its name gradually evolved from 'papa' to 'battata'. It became famous not only for its nutritional value, but also for its healing properties.

The Italians believed that the cooked flesh would heal a wound if rubbed into the infected area, and Pope Pious IV was sufficiently convinced of this to plant his own crop in Italy. From here, the potato moved northwards through Switzerland, France, Germany and Belgium, reaching the New World with the explorer Frances Drake, who shared his cargo of potatoes with the starving English colonists. Sir Walter Raleigh later brought the potato to Britain. He also took it to Ireland, where the soil was perfect for growing it, and it became a dietary mainstay for the Irish peasantry, who survived for generations on very little else.

Nutritionally, potatoes are an excellent source of starch for energy and fibre. They have a higher protein value than most plant foods, are very rich in vitamin C, and also contain vitamin B-complex, as well as minerals, especially potassium. However, many of the nutrients are found in or just below the skin, so it is essential to cook them in ways that will retain their health-promoting properties.

Although potatoes were once considered to be forbidden to slimmers, they are in fact a positive aid to weight control when cooked and served with the minimum of fat. Sufferers from stomach ulcers and arthritis will also benefit from drinking raw potato juice, although their taste buds may object to the flavour!

This book is a collection of some of the most delicious and diverse potato recipes, which have been gathered from around the world. Whatever the occasion, these dishes will show you how this splendidly adaptable vegetable can be used in a multitude of ways to enhance your everyday eating.

Regional Cooking

Although the potato is known and grown throughout the world, the ways in which it is cooked and served vary enormously from country to country, and often depend on whether it is the main staple of a nation's diet.

The highest consumers are Russia, Poland and Germany, followed by Holland, Cyprus and Ireland. Elsewhere the potato may be used less than pasta, rice, or bread in the daily diet.

As Spain was the first European country to discover the potato, it is appropriate that it is used in one of the most popular and well-known classic Spanish dishes, tortilla, a substantial, crispy-coated vegetable omelette based on eggs and thinly sliced waxy potatoes, to which may be added peppers, tomatoes, sweetcorn – the choice is unlimited. Variations of this recipe can be found all around the Mediterranean – a Greek version, for example, involves filling the potato omelette with a melting mixture of feta cheese and spinach.

In Italy, floury potatoes are used in another classic dish – gnocchi. Here, the cooked potatoes are mixed with flour, egg yolks and olive oil to make little dumplings, which are cooked in boiling water and served with a sauce. Herbs or cheese may be added to the basic recipe, and a delicious variation is to add spinach. A similar base can also be used to make potato noodles.

From Ireland comes Colcannon – a wonderful mixture of mashed potatoes and shredded cabbage, topped with a pool of melted butter – which is usually served with a piece of cooked bacon.

Regional Cooking

Worldwide, the potato is often used as a basis for a hearty salad. On the Mediterranean coast of France, potatoes are combined with tuna and eggs as the base for the famous Salade Niçoise. In India, they may be mixed with broccoli and mango, and topped with a spicy yoghurt dressing, while in Mexico sliced potatoes are topped with tomatoes, chillies and ham and served with guacamole. In Italy, potatoes are layered with sausage, raddichio, sun-dried tomatoes and basil and drizzled with a tomato-flavoured olive oil dressing, and in Russia the classic combination of cucumber and dill can be made more substantial by the addition of potatoes and beetroot.

The potato makes an excellent ingredient in soups, and in European cuisine, potatoes are used in a number of classic soup recipes – Vichyssoise, Pistou, and Bouillabaisse, to name just a few. Different cultures also have their own variations of chowder, a filling soup based on potatoes and milk. In New England, for example, fresh clams are added, while in Scotland the chowder is flavoured with smoked haddock to make the intriguingly named Cullen Skink.

Even as an accompaniment, potatoes are served in a variety of ways. In India, for example, they are mixed with other vegetables, which readily absorb the curry flavours. In France, layers of waxy potatoes are topped with double cream and sometimes cheese to make Potatoes Dauphinois. In Britain, they are served roasted to a crisp with the traditional Sunday lunch, and in Belgium potato chips are usually served accompanied by mayonnaise, for dipping.

How to Use This Book

Each recipe contains a wealth of useful information, including a breakdown of nutritional quantities, preparation and cooking times, and level of difficulty. All of this information is explained in detail below.

● This amount of time represents the actual cooking time.

The nutritional information provided for each recipe is per serving or per portion. Optional ingredients, variations or serving suggestions have not been included in the calculations. ●

The number of chef's ● hats represents the difficulty of each recipe, ranging from easy (1 chef's hat) to difficult (5 chef's hats).

This amount of ● time represents the preparation of ingredients, including cooling, chilling and soaking times.

The ingredients for ● each recipe are listed in the order that they are used.

● The method is clearly explained with step-by-step instructions that are easy to follow.

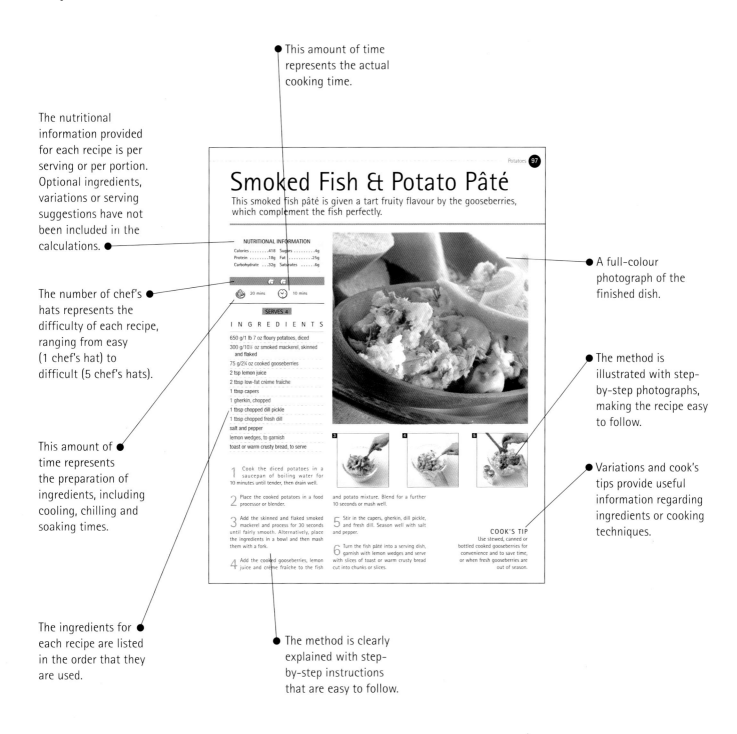

Potatoes 97

Smoked Fish & Potato Pâté
This smoked fish pâté is given a tart fruity flavour by the gooseberries, which complement the fish perfectly.

NUTRITIONAL INFORMATION

Calories . . . . .418 Sugars 4g
Protein . . . . .18g Fat 25g
Carbohydrate . . .32g Saturates 6g

20 mins   10 mins

SERVES 4

I N G R E D I E N T S

650 g/1 lb 7 oz floury potatoes, diced
300 g/10½ oz smoked mackerel, skinned and flaked
75 g/2¾ oz cooked gooseberries
2 tsp lemon juice
2 tbsp low-fat crème fraîche
1 tbsp capers
1 gherkin, chopped
1 tbsp chopped dill pickle
1 tbsp chopped fresh dill
salt and pepper
lemon wedges, to garnish
toast or warm crusty bread, to serve

1 Cook the diced potatoes in a saucepan of boiling water for 10 minutes until tender, then drain well.

2 Place the cooked potatoes in a food processor or blender.

3 Add the skinned and flaked smoked mackerel and process for 30 seconds until fairly smooth. Alternatively, place the ingredients in a bowl and then mash them with a fork.

4 Add the cooked gooseberries, lemon juice and crème fraîche to the fish and potato mixture. Blend for a further 10 seconds or mash well.

5 Stir in the capers, gherkin, dill pickle, and fresh dill. Season well with salt and pepper.

6 Turn the fish pâté into a serving dish, garnish with lemon wedges and serve with slices of toast or warm crusty bread cut into chunks or slices.

COOK'S TIP
Use stewed, canned or bottled cooked gooseberries for convenience and to save time, or when fresh gooseberries are out of season.

● A full-colour photograph of the finished dish.

● The method is illustrated with step-by-step photographs, making the recipe easy to follow.

● Variations and cook's tips provide useful information regarding ingredients or cooking techniques.

Soups, Starters & Salads

Potatoes form the basis of many delicious and easy-to-prepare home-made soups, because they are the perfect thickening agent while adding a subtle flavour. With the addition of just a few ingredients, you can have a selection of soups at your fingertips.

Also featured in this chapter are starters and salads based on potatoes. In addition to the creamy potato salads that are so popular, there are many other recipes to tempt your palate, including dishes suitable for light lunches as well as hearty main-course meals. Many are also ideal for barbecues and picnics.

Creamy Sweetcorn Soup

This filling combination of tender sweetcorn kernels and a creamy stock is extra delicious with lean diced ham sprinkled on top.

NUTRITIONAL INFORMATION

Calories . . . . .307 Sugars 15g
Protein . . . . .19g Fat 14g
Carbohydrate . . .28g Saturates 5g

15 mins   25 mins

SERVES 4

INGREDIENTS

1 large onion, chopped

300 g/10½ oz potatoes, diced

1 litre/1¾ pints skimmed milk

1 bay leaf

½ tsp ground nutmeg

450 g/1 lb sweetcorn kernels, canned or frozen, drained or thawed

1 tbsp cornflour

3 tbsp cold water

4 tbsp natural low-fat yogurt

salt and pepper

TO GARNISH

100 g/3½ oz lean ham, diced

2 tbsp fresh chives, snipped

1 Place the onion and potato in a large saucepan and pour over the milk.

2 Add the bay leaf, nutmeg and half the sweetcorn to the saucepan. Bring to the boil, cover and simmer gently for 15 minutes until the potato is softened. Stir the soup occasionally and keep the heat low so that the milk does not burn on the bottom of the pan.

3 Discard the bay leaf and leave the liquid to cool for 10 minutes. Transfer to a blender and process for a few seconds. Alternatively, rub the soup through a sieve.

4 Pour the smooth liquid into a saucepan. Blend the cornflour with the cold water to make a paste and stir it into the soup.

5 Bring the soup back to the boil, stirring until it thickens, and add the remaining sweetcorn. Heat through for 2–3 minutes until piping hot.

6 Remove the soup from the heat and season well with salt and pepper to taste. Stir in the yogurt until it is thoroughly blended.

7 Ladle the creamy sweetcorn soup into warm bowls and serve sprinkled with the diced ham and snipped chives.

Sweet Potato & Onion Soup

This simple recipe uses the sweet potato with its distinctive flavour and colour, combined with a hint of orange and coriander.

NUTRITIONAL INFORMATION

Calories 320	Sugars 26g
Protein 7g	Fat 7g
Carbohydrate ...62g	Saturates 1g

15 mins   30 mins

SERVES 4

INGREDIENTS

2 tbsp vegetable oil

900 g/2 lb sweet potatoes, diced

1 carrot, diced

2 onions, sliced

2 garlic cloves, crushed

600 ml/1 pint vegetable stock

300 ml/10 fl oz unsweetened orange juice

225 ml/8 fl oz low-fat natural yogurt

2 tbsp chopped fresh coriander

salt and pepper

TO GARNISH

coriander sprigs

orange rind

1 Heat the vegetable oil in a large saucepan and add the sweet potatoes, carrot, onions and garlic. Sauté the vegetables gently for 5 minutes, stirring constantly.

2 Pour in the vegetable stock and orange juice and bring them to the boil.

3 Reduce the heat to a simmer, cover the saucepan and cook the vegetables for 20 minutes or until the sweet potatoes and carrot are tender.

4 Transfer the mixture to a food processor or blender in batches and process for 1 minute until puréed. Return the purée to the rinsed-out saucepan.

5 Stir in the yogurt and chopped coriander and season to taste.

6 Serve the soup in warm bowls and garnish with coriander sprigs and orange rind.

VARIATION

This soup can be chilled before serving, if preferred. If chilling, stir the yogurt into the dish just before serving. Serve in chilled bowls.

Potato & Chickpea Soup

This spicy and substantial soup uses ingredients you are likely to have on hand and makes a delicious meal-in-a-bowl.

NUTRITIONAL INFORMATION

Calories	40	Sugars	.......1.6g
Protein	........1.8g	Fat	...........1g
Carbohydrate	...6.5g	Saturates	.....0.1g

5 mins 50 mins

SERVES 4

INGREDIENTS

1 tbsp olive oil

1 large onion, finely chopped

2–3 garlic cloves, finely chopped or crushed

1 carrot, quartered and thinly sliced

350 g/12 oz potatoes, diced

¼ tsp ground turmeric

¼ tsp garam masala

¼ tsp mild curry powder

400 g/14 oz canned chopped tomatoes in juice

850 ml/1½ pints water

¼ tsp chilli purée, or to taste

400 g/14 oz canned chickpeas, rinsed and drained

85 g/3 oz fresh or frozen peas

salt and pepper

chopped fresh coriander, to garnish

1 Heat the olive oil in a large saucepan over a medium heat. Add the onion and garlic and cook for 3–4 minutes, stirring occasionally, until the onion is beginning to soften.

2 Add the carrot, potatoes, turmeric, garam masala and curry powder and continue cooking for 1–2 minutes.

3 Add the tomatoes, water and chilli purée with a large pinch of salt.

Reduce the heat, cover and simmer for 30 minutes, stirring occasionally.

4 Add the chickpeas and peas to the pan, then continue cooking for about 15 minutes, or until all the vegetables are tender.

5 Taste the soup and adjust the seasoning, if necessary, adding a little more chilli if desired. Ladle into warm soup bowls and sprinkle with coriander.

Potato, Apple & Rocket Soup

Rocket is a fashionable salad leaf that has a slightly bitter flavour.
It also gives a delicate green colouring to this soup.

NUTRITIONAL INFORMATION

Calories 59   Sugars 2.7g
Protein ....20g   Fat 2g
Carbohydrate ...8.5g Saturates 1.2g

5 mins   35 mins

SERVES 4

INGREDIENTS

4 tbsp butter

900 g/2 lb waxy potatoes, diced

1 red onion, quartered

1 tbsp lemon juice

1 litre/1¾ pints chicken stock

450 g/1 lb dessert apples, peeled and diced

pinch of ground allspice

50 g/1¾ oz rocket leaves

salt and pepper

TO GARNISH

slices of red apple

chopped spring onions

1 Melt the butter in a large saucepan and add the diced potatoes and sliced red onion. Sauté gently for 5 minutes, stirring constantly.

2 Add the lemon juice, chicken stock, apples and ground allspice.

3 Bring to the boil, then reduce the heat to a simmer, cover the pan and cook for 15 minutes.

4 Add the rocket to the soup and cook for a further 10 minutes until the potatoes are cooked through.

5 Transfer half of the soup to a food processor or blender and process for 1 minute. Return to the pan and stir the purée into the remaining soup.

6 Season to taste with salt and pepper. Ladle the soup into warmed soup bowls and garnish with the apple slices and chopped spring onions. Serve at once with warm crusty bread.

COOK'S TIP

If rocket is unavailable, use baby spinach instead for a similar flavour.

Indian Potato & Pea Soup

A slightly hot and spicy Indian flavour is given to this soup with the use of garam masala, chilli, cumin and coriander.

NUTRITIONAL INFORMATION

Calories	160	Sugars	.........8g
Protein	.........6g	Fat	...........7g
Carbohydrate	...21g	Saturates	.......1g

 5 mins   35 mins

SERVES 4

INGREDIENTS

2 tbsp vegetable oil

225 g/8 oz floury potatoes, diced

1 large onion, chopped

2 garlic cloves, crushed

1 tsp garam masala

1 tsp ground coriander

1 tsp ground cumin

850 ml/1½ pints vegetable stock

1 red chilli, chopped

100 g/3½ oz frozen peas

4 tbsp natural yogurt

salt and pepper

chopped coriander, to garnish

warm bread, to serve

VARIATION

For slightly less heat, deseed the chilli before adding it to the soup. Always wash your hands after handling chillies because they contain volatile oils that can irritate the skin and make your eyes burn if you touch your face.

1 Heat the vegetable oil in a large saucepan. Add the potatoes, onion and garlic and sauté over a low heat, stirring constantly, for about 5 minutes.

2 Add the garam masala, coriander and cumin and cook, stirring constantly, for 1 minute.

3 Stir in the vegetable stock and red chilli and bring the mixture to the boil. Reduce the heat, cover the pan and simmer for 20 minutes, until the potatoes begin to break down.

4 Add the peas and cook for a further 5 minutes. Stir in the yogurt and season to taste with salt and pepper.

5 Pour into warmed soup bowls, garnish with chopped fresh coriander and serve hot with warm bread.

Broccoli & Potato Soup

This creamy soup has a delightful pale green colouring and rich flavour from the blend of tender broccoli and blue cheese.

NUTRITIONAL INFORMATION

Calories 452	Sugars 4g	
Protein 14g	Fat 35g	
Carbohydrate ...20g	Saturates 19g	

 5–10 mins 35 mins

SERVES 4

INGREDIENTS

2 tbsp olive oil

450 g/1 lb potatoes, diced

1 onion, diced

225 g/8 oz broccoli florets

125 g/4½ oz blue cheese, crumbled

1 litre/1¾ pints vegetable stock

150 m/5 fl oz double cream

pinch of paprika

salt and pepper

1 Heat the oil in a large saucepan. Add the potatoes and onion. Sauté, stirring constantly, for 5 minutes.

2 Reserve a few broccoli florets for the garnish and add the remaining broccoli to the pan. Add the cheese and vegetable stock.

3 Bring to the boil, then reduce the heat, cover the pan and simmer for 25 minutes, until the potatoes are tender.

4 Transfer the soup to a food processor or blender in batches and process until the mixture is smooth. Alternatively, press the vegetables through a strainer with the back of a wooden spoon.

5 Return the purée to a clean saucepan and stir in the double cream and a pinch of paprika. Season to taste with salt and pepper.

6 Blanch the reserved broccoli florets in a little boiling water for about 2 minutes, then lift them out of the pan with a slotted spoon.

7 Pour the soup into warmed individual bowls and garnish with the broccoli florets and a sprinkling of paprika. Serve the soup immediately.

COOK'S TIP

This soup freezes very successfully. Follow the method described here up to step 4, and freeze the soup after it has been puréed. Add the cream and paprika just before serving. Garnish and serve.

Potato & Mushroom Soup

There are many varieties of dried mushrooms available on the market today; the concentrated flavour they add to a dish justifies the cost.

NUTRITIONAL INFORMATION

Calories . . . . .81 Sugars 0.7g
Protein . . . . .3.8g Fat 4g
Carbohydrate . . .7.6g Saturates 1.8g

5 mins · 30 mins

SERVES 4

INGREDIENTS

2 tbsp vegetable oil

600 g/1 lb 5 oz floury potatoes, sliced

1 onion, sliced

2 garlic cloves, crushed

1 litre/1¾ pints beef stock

25 g/1 oz dried mushrooms

2 celery sticks, sliced

2 tbsp brandy

salt and pepper

TOPPING

3 tbsp butter

2 thick slices white bread, crusts removed

50 g/1¾ oz Parmesan cheese,
   freshly grated

TO GARNISH

rehydrated dried mushrooms

parsley sprigs

COOK'S TIP

Probably the most popular dried mushroom is the cep, but any variety will add a lovely flavour to this soup. If you do not wish to use dried mushrooms, add 125 g/4½ oz sliced fresh mushrooms of your choice to the soup.

1 Heat the vegetable oil in a large frying pan and add the potatoes, onion and garlic. Sauté gently for 5 minutes, stirring constantly.

2 Add the beef stock, dried mushrooms of your choice, and the celery. Bring to the boil, then reduce the heat to a simmer, cover the saucepan and continue to cook the soup for 20 minutes until the potatoes are tender.

3 Meanwhile, melt the butter for the topping in the frying pan. Sprinkle the bread slices with the grated cheese and fry the slices in the butter for 1 minute on each side until crisp. Using a sharp knife, cut each slice into triangles.

4 Stir the brandy into the soup, and season to taste. Pour into warmed bowls and top with the triangles. Serve garnished with mushrooms and parsley.

Potato & Split Pea Soup

Split green peas are sweeter than other varieties of split pea and reduce down to a purée when cooked, which acts as a thickener in soups.

NUTRITIONAL INFORMATION

Calories	260	Sugars	.........5g
Protein	........11g	Fat	..........10g
Carbohydrate	...32g	Saturates	.......3g

 5–10 mins 45 mins

SERVES 4

INGREDIENTS

2 tbsp vegetable oil

450 g/1 lb unpeeled floury potatoes, diced

2 onions, diced

75 g/2¾ oz split green peas

1 litre/1¾ pints vegetable stock

60 g/2¼ oz Gruyère cheese, grated

salt and pepper

CROÛTONS

3 tbsp butter

1 garlic clove, crushed

1 tbsp chopped parsley

1 thick slice white bread, cubed

1 Heat the vegetable oil in a large saucepan. Add the potatoes and onions and sauté over a low heat, stirring constantly, for about 5 minutes.

VARIATION

For a richly coloured soup, red lentils could be used instead of split green peas. Add a large pinch of brown sugar to the recipe for extra sweetness if red lentils are used.

2 Add the split green peas to the pan and stir together well.

3 Pour the vegetable stock into the pan and bring to the boil. Reduce the heat to low and simmer for 35 minutes, until the potatoes are tender and the split peas are cooked.

4 Meanwhile, make the croûtons. Melt the butter in a frying pan. Add the garlic, parsley and bread cubes and cook, turning frequently, for about 2 minutes, until the bread cubes are golden brown on all sides.

5 Stir the grated cheese into the soup and season to taste with salt and pepper. Heat gently until the cheese is starting to melt.

6 Pour the soup into warmed individual bowls and sprinkle the croûtons on top. Serve at once.

Vegetable & Corn Chowder

This is a really filling soup, which should be served before a light main course. It is easy to prepare and filled with flavour.

NUTRITIONAL INFORMATION

Calories 378	Sugars 20g
Protein 16g	Fat 13g
Carbohydrate ...52g	Saturates 6g

 15 mins   30 mins

SERVES 4

I N G R E D I E N T S

1 tbsp vegetable oil

1 red onion, diced

1 red pepper, deseeded and diced

3 garlic cloves, crushed

300 g/10½ oz potatoes, diced

2 tbsp plain flour

600 ml milk

300 ml/10 fl oz vegetable stock

50 g/1¾ oz broccoli florets

300 g/10½ oz canned sweetcorn, drained

75 g/2¾ oz Cheddar cheese, grated

salt and pepper

1 tbsp chopped fresh coriander, to garnish

COOK'S TIP

Vegetarian cheeses are made with rennets of non-animal origin, using microbial or fungal enzymes.

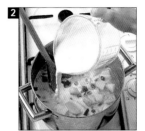

1 Heat the oil in a large saucepan. Add the onion, red pepper, garlic and potatoes and sauté over a low heat, stirring frequently, for 2–3 minutes.

2 Stir in the flour and cook, stirring, for 30 seconds. Gradually stir in the milk and stock.

3 Add the broccoli and sweetcorn. Bring the mixture to the boil, stirring constantly, then reduce the heat and simmer for about 20 minutes, or until all the vegetables are tender.

4 Stir in 50 g/1¾ oz of the cheese until it melts.

5 Season to taste, then spoon the chowder into a warm soup tureen. Garnish with the remaining cheese and the coriander and serve.

Broad Bean & Mint Soup

Fresh broad beans are best for this scrumptious soup, but if they are unavailable, use frozen beans instead.

NUTRITIONAL INFORMATION

Calories ....224 Sugars 4g
Protein ....12g Fat 6g
Carbohydrate ...31g Saturates 1g

 15 mins   40 mins

SERVES 4

INGREDIENTS

2 tbsp olive oil

1 red onion, chopped

2 garlic cloves, crushed

450 g/1 lb potatoes, diced

500 g/1 lb 2 oz broad beans,
  thawed if frozen

850 ml/1½ pints vegetable stock

2 tbsp freshly chopped mint

mint sprigs and natural yogurt, to garnish

1 Heat the olive oil in a large saucepan. Add the onion and garlic and sauté for 2–3 minutes, until softened.

2 Add the potatoes and cook, stirring constantly, for 5 minutes.

3 Stir in the beans and the stock, then cover the pan and simmer for 30 minutes, or until the beans and potatoes are tender.

4 Remove a few vegetables with a slotted spoon and set aside. Place the remainder of the soup in a food processor or blender and process until smooth.

5 Return the soup to a clean saucepan and add the reserved vegetables and chopped mint. Stir thoroughly and heat through gently.

6 Transfer the soup to a warm tureen or individual serving bowls. Garnish with swirls of yogurt and sprigs of fresh mint and serve immediately.

VARIATION
Use fresh coriander and ½ teaspoon ground cumin as flavourings in the soup, if you prefer.

Sweet Potato & Squash Soup

When there's a chill in the air, this vivid soup is just the thing to serve – it's very warm and comforting.

NUTRITIONAL INFORMATION

Calories 57   Sugars 1.5g
Protein ....2.3g   Fat 2.5g
Carbohydrate ...6.6g   Saturates 0.8g

15 mins   1 hr 15 mins

SERVES 6

I N G R E D I E N T S

350 g/12 oz sweet potatoes

1 acorn squash

4 shallots

olive oil

5–6 garlic cloves, unpeeled

850 ml/1½ pints chicken stock

125 ml/4 fl oz single cream

salt and pepper

snipped chives, to garnish

1 Cut the sweet potatoes, squash and shallots in half lengthways. Brush the cut sides with oil.

2 Put the vegetables, cut sides down, in a shallow roasting tin. Add the garlic cloves. Roast in a preheated oven at 190°C/375°F/Gas Mark 5 for about 40 minutes until tender and light brown.

3 When cool, scoop the flesh from the potato and squash halves and put in a saucepan with the shallots. Remove the garlic peel and add the soft insides to the other vegetables.

4 Add the stock and a pinch of salt. Bring just to the boil, reduce the heat and simmer, partially covered, for about 30 minutes, stirring occasionally, until the vegetables are very tender.

5 Allow the soup to cool slightly, then transfer to a blender or food processor and purée until smooth, working in batches, if necessary. (If using a food processor, strain off the cooking liquid and reserve. Purée the soup solids with enough cooking liquid to moisten them, then combine with the remaining liquid.)

6 Return the soup to the saucepan and stir in the cream. Season to taste, then simmer for 5–10 minutes until completely heated through. Ladle into warm bowls to serve.

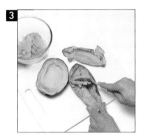

Celeriac, Leek & Potato Soup

It is hard to imagine that celeriac, a coarse, knobbly vegetable, can taste so sweet. It makes a wonderfully flavoursome soup.

NUTRITIONAL INFORMATION

Calories	20	Sugars	.......1.3g
Protein	........0.8g	Fat	..........0.7g
Carbohydrate	...2.7g	Saturates	.....0.4g

🕙 10 mins   🕐 35 mins

SERVES 4

I N G R E D I E N T S

1 tbsp butter

1 onion, chopped

2 large leeks, halved lengthways and sliced

750 g/1 lb 10 oz celeriac, peeled and cubed

225 g/8 oz potatoes, cubed

1 carrot, quartered and thinly sliced

1.2 litres/2 pints water

⅛ tsp dried marjoram

1 bay leaf

freshly grated nutmeg

salt and pepper

celery leaves, to garnish

1 Melt the butter in a large saucepan over a medium–low heat. Add the onion and leeks and cook for about 4 minutes, stirring frequently, until just softened; do not allow to colour.

2 Add the celeriac, potatoes, carrot, water, marjoram and bay leaf, with a large pinch of salt. Bring to the boil, reduce the heat, cover and simmer for about 25 minutes until the vegetables are tender. Remove the bay leaf.

3 Allow the soup to cool slightly. Transfer to a blender or food processor and purée until smooth. (If using a food processor, strain off the cooking liquid and reserve. Purée the soup solids with enough cooking liquid to moisten them, then combine with the remaining liquid.)

4 Return the puréed soup to the saucepan and stir to blend the ingredients thoroughly. Season the soup with nutmeg, salt and pepper to taste, then simmer over a medium–low heat until reheated.

5 Ladle the soup into warm bowls, garnish with celery leaves and then serve immediately.

Roasted Garlic & Potato Soup

The combination of potato, garlic and onion works brilliantly in soup. In this recipe the garlic is roasted to give it added dimension and depth.

NUTRITIONAL INFORMATION

Calories ....240 Sugars 7g
Protein ....8g Fat 10g
Carbohydrate ...33g Saturates 5g

10 mins · 1 hr

SERVES 4

I N G R E D I E N T S

1 large bulb of garlic with large cloves, peeled (about 100 g/3½ oz)

2 tsp olive oil

2 large leeks, thinly sliced

1 large onion, finely chopped

500 g/1 lb 2 oz potatoes, diced

1.2 litres/2 pints chicken or vegetable stock

1 bay leaf

150 ml/5 fl oz single cream

freshly grated nutmeg

fresh lemon juice, optional

salt and pepper

snipped fresh chives or parsley, to garnish

1 Put the garlic cloves in a baking dish, lightly brush with oil and bake in a preheated oven at 180°C/350°F/Gas Mark 4 for about 20 minutes until golden.

2 Heat the oil in a large saucepan over a medium heat. Add the leeks and onion, cover and cook for about 3 minutes, stirring frequently, until they begin to soften.

3 Add the potatoes, roasted garlic, stock and bay leaf. Season with salt (unless the stock is salty already) and pepper. Bring to the boil, reduce the heat, cover and cook gently for about 30 minutes until the vegetables are tender. Remove the bay leaf.

4 Allow the soup to cool slightly, then transfer to a blender or food processor and purée until smooth, working in batches if necessary. (If using a food processor, strain off the cooking liquid and reserve. Purée the soup solids with enough cooking liquid to moisten them, then combine with the remaining liquid.)

5 Return the soup to the saucepan and stir in the cream and a generous grating of nutmeg. Taste and adjust the seasoning, if necessary, adding a few drops of lemon juice, if desired. Reheat over a low heat. Ladle into warm soup bowls, garnish with chives or parsley and serve.

Sweet Potato & Apple Soup

This soup makes a marvellous late autumn or winter starter. It has a delicious texture and cheerful golden colour.

NUTRITIONAL INFORMATION

Calories 57	Sugars 3.8g	
Protein 0.7g	Fat 2.9g	
Carbohydrate ...7.4g	Saturates 1.8g	

🥔 10 mins   🕙 45 mins

SERVES 6

I N G R E D I E N T S

1 tbsp butter

3 leeks, thinly sliced

1 large carrot, thinly sliced

600 g/1 lb 5 oz sweet potatoes, peeled and cubed

2 large, tart eating apples, peeled and cubed

I.2 litres/2 pints water

freshly grated nutmeg

225 ml/8 fl oz apple juice

225 ml/8 fl oz single cream

salt and pepper

snipped fresh chives or coriander, to garnish

1 Melt the butter in a large saucepan over a medium–low heat. Add the leeks, cover and cook for 6–8 minutes, or until softened, stirring frequently.

2 Add the carrot, sweet potatoes, apples and water. Season lightly with salt, pepper and nutmeg to taste. Bring to the boil, reduce the heat and simmer, covered, for about 20 minutes, stirring occasionally, until the vegetables are very tender.

3 Allow the soup to cool slightly, then transfer to a blender or food processor and purée until smooth, working in batches if necessary. (If using a food processor, strain off the cooking liquid and reserve. Purée the soup solids with enough cooking liquid to moisten them, then combine with the remaining liquid.)

4 Return the puréed soup to the saucepan and stir in the apple juice.

Place over a low heat and simmer for about 10 minutes until heated through.

5 Stir in the cream and continue simmering for about 5 minutes, stirring frequently, until heated through. Taste and adjust the seasoning, adding more salt, pepper and nutmeg, if necessary. Ladle the soup into warm bowls, garnish with chives or coriander and serve.

Vichyssoise

This is a classic creamy soup made from potatoes and leeks. To achieve the delicate pale colour, be sure to use only the white parts of the leeks.

NUTRITIONAL INFORMATION

Calories 208   Sugars 5g
Protein . . . . .5g   Fat 12g
Carbohydrate . . .20g   Saturates 6g

10 mins   40 mins

SERVES 6

I N G R E D I E N T S

3 large leeks

3 tbsp butter or margarine

1 onion, thinly sliced

500 g/1 lb 2 oz potatoes, chopped

850 ml/1½ pints vegetable stock

2 tsp lemon juice

pinch of ground nutmeg

¼ tsp ground coriander

1 bay leaf

1 egg yolk

150 ml/5 fl oz single cream

salt and pepper

freshly snipped chives, to garnish

1 Trim the leeks and remove most of the green parts. Slice the white parts of the leeks very finely.

2 Melt the butter or margarine in a saucepan. Add the leeks and onion and fry, stirring occasionally, for about 5 minutes without browning.

3 Add the potatoes, vegetable stock, lemon juice, nutmeg, coriander and bay leaf to the pan, season to taste with salt and pepper and bring to the boil. Cover and simmer for about 30 minutes, until all the vegetables are very soft.

4 Cool the soup a little, remove and discard the bay leaf and then press through a sieve or process in a food processor or blender until smooth. Pour into a clean pan.

5 Blend the egg yolk into the cream, add a little of the soup to the mixture and then whisk it all back into the soup and reheat gently, without boiling. Adjust the seasoning to taste. Leave to cool and then chill thoroughly in the refrigerator.

6 Serve the soup sprinkled with freshly snipped chives.

Watercress Vichyssoise

Vichyssoise is simply cold leek and potato soup flavoured with chives. The addition of watercress gives it a cool, refreshing flavour and lovely colour.

NUTRITIONAL INFORMATION

Calories 42	Sugars 0.8g
Protein 2.1g	Fat 2.2g
Carbohydrate . . .3.6g	Saturates 1g

 15 mins   35 mins

SERVES 6

I N G R E D I E N T S

1 tbsp olive oil

3 large leeks, thinly sliced

350 g/12 oz potatoes, finely diced

600 ml/1 pint chicken or vegetable stock

450 ml/16 fl oz water

1 bay leaf

175 g/6 oz prepared watercress

175 ml/6 fl oz single cream

salt and pepper

watercress leaves, to garnish

1 Heat the oil in a heavy-based saucepan over a medium heat. Add the sliced leeks and cook for about 3 minutes, stirring frequently, until they begin to soften.

2 Add the potatoes, stock, water and bay leaf. Add salt if the stock is unsalted. Bring to the boil, then reduce the heat, cover the saucepan and cook gently for about 25 minutes, until the vegetables are tender. Remove the bay leaf and discard it.

3 Add the watercress and continue to cook for a further 2–3 minutes, stirring frequently, until the watercress is completely wilted.

4 Allow the soup to cool slightly, then transfer to a blender or food processor and purée until smooth, working in batches if necessary. (If using a food processor, strain off the cooking liquid and reserve. Purée the soup solids with enough cooking liquid to moisten them, then combine with the remaining liquid.)

5 Put the soup into a large bowl and then stir in half the cream. Season with salt, if needed, and plenty of pepper. Leave to cool to room temperature.

6 Refrigerate until cold. Taste and adjust the seasoning, if necessary. Ladle into chilled bowls, drizzle the remaining cream on top and garnish with watercress leaves. Serve at once.

Mixed Fish Soup

Any mixture of fish is suitable for this recipe, from simple smoked and white fish to salmon or mussels, depending on the occasion.

NUTRITIONAL INFORMATION

Calories ....458 Sugars 5g
Protein ....28g Fat 25g
Carbohydrate ...22g Saturates 12g

 10 mins   35 mins

SERVES 4

INGREDIENTS

2 tbsp vegetable oil

450 g/1 lb small new potatoes, halved

1 bunch spring onions, sliced

1 yellow pepper, sliced

2 garlic cloves, crushed

225 ml/8 fl oz dry white wine

600 ml/1 pint fish stock

225 g/8 oz white fish fillet, skinned and cubed

225 g/8 oz smoked cod fillet, skinned and cubed

2 tomatoes, peeled, deseeded and chopped

100 g/3½ oz peeled cooked prawns

150 ml/5 fl oz double cream

2 tbsp shredded fresh basil

1 Heat the vegetable oil in a large saucepan and add the halved potatoes, spring onions, pepper and garlic. Sauté gently for 3 minutes, stirring constantly.

2 Add the white wine and fish stock and bring to the boil. Reduce the heat and simmer for 10-15 minutes.

3 Add the fish fillet cubes and chopped tomatoes and continue to cook for 10 minutes or until the fish is cooked through completely.

4 Stir in the cooked prawns, the cream and the shredded basil and cook for 2-3 minutes. Pour the soup into warmed bowls and serve immediately.

COOK'S TIP

For a soup that is slightly less rich, omit the wine and stir natural yogurt into the soup instead of the double cream.

Smoked Haddock Soup

This chunky, aromatic soup is perfect for a cold weather lunch or supper served with crusty bread and a salad.

NUTRITIONAL INFORMATION

Calories 80	Sugars 2.9g	
Protein 4.3g	Fat 3g	
Carbohydrate ...9.6g	Saturates 1.4g	

5–10 mins   40 mins

SERVES 4

INGREDIENTS

1 tbsp oil

55 g/2 oz smoked streaky bacon, cut into matchsticks

1 large onion, finely chopped

2 tbsp plain flour

1 litre/1¾ pints milk

700 g/1 lb 9 oz potatoes, cubed

175 g/6 oz skinless smoked haddock

salt and pepper

finely chopped fresh parsley, to garnish

1 Heat the oil in a large saucepan over a medium heat. Add the bacon and cook for 2 minutes. Stir in the onion and continue cooking for 5–7 minutes, stirring frequently, until the onion is soft and the bacon golden. Tip the pan and spoon off as much fat as possible.

2 Stir in the flour and continue cooking for 2 minutes. Add half of the milk and stir well, scraping the bottom of the pan to mix in the flour.

3 Add the potatoes and remaining milk and season with pepper. Bring just to the boil, stirring frequently, then reduce the heat and simmer, partially covered, for 10 minutes.

4 Add the fish and continue cooking, stirring occasionally, for about 15 minutes, or until the potatoes are tender and the fish breaks up easily.

5 Taste the soup and adjust the seasoning if necessary (salt may not be needed). Ladle into a warm tureen or soup bowls and sprinkle generously with chopped parsley.

COOK'S TIP

Cutting the potatoes into small cubes not only looks attractive, it allows them to cook more quickly and evenly.

Breton Fish Soup with Cider

Fishermen's soups are variable, depending on the season and the catch. Monkfish has a texture like lobster, but tender cod is equally appealing.

NUTRITIONAL INFORMATION

Calories 103	Sugars 1.5g
Protein 5.2g	Fat 6.3g
Carbohydrate . . .6.6g	Saturates 3.8g

5–10 mins   40 mins

SERVES 4

INGREDIENTS

2 tsp butter

1 large leek, thinly sliced

2 shallots, finely chopped

300ml/10 fl oz cider

125 ml/4 fl oz fish stock

250 g/9 oz potatoes, diced

1 bay leaf

4 tbsp plain flour

175 ml/6 fl oz milk

175 ml/6 fl oz double cream

55 g/2 oz fresh sorrel leaves

350 g/12 oz skinless monkfish or cod fillet, cut into 2.5-cm/1-inch pieces

salt and pepper

COOK'S TIP

Be careful not to overcook the fish, otherwise tender fish, such as cod, breaks up into smaller and smaller flakes, and firm fish, such as monkfish, can become tough.

1 Melt the butter in a large saucepan over a medium-low heat. Add the leek and shallots and cook for about 5 minutes, stirring frequently, until they start to soften. Add the cider and bring to the boil.

2 Stir in the stock, potatoes and bay leaf with a large pinch of salt (unless stock is salty) and bring back to the boil. Reduce the heat, cover and cook gently for 10 minutes.

3 Put the flour in a small bowl and very slowly whisk in a few tablespoons of the milk to make a thick paste. Stir in a little more milk, if needed, to make a smooth liquid.

4 Adjust the heat so that the soup bubbles gently. Stir in the flour mixture and cook, stirring frequently, for 5 minutes. Add the remaining milk and half the cream. Continue cooking for about 10 minutes until the potatoes are tender.

5 Chop the sorrel finely and combine with the remaining cream. (If using a food processor, add the sorrel and chop, then add the cream and process briefly.)

6 Stir the sorrel cream into the soup and add the fish. Continue cooking, stirring occasionally, for about 3 minutes, until the monkfish stiffens or the cod just begins to flake. Taste the soup and adjust the seasoning, if necessary. Ladle into warm bowls and serve.

Fennel & Tomato Soup

This light and refreshing soup is also good served cold. An ideal starter for a summer meal, served with crunchy Melba toast.

NUTRITIONAL INFORMATION

Calories	110	Sugars	. . . . .8g
Protein	. . . . .10g	Fat	. . . . .2g
Carbohydrate	. . .13g	Saturates	. . . . . . .0g

 30 mins   40 mins

SERVES 4

INGREDIENTS

2 tsp olive oil

1 large onion, halved and sliced

2 large fennel bulbs, halved and sliced

1 small potato, diced

850 ml/1½ pints water

400 ml/14 fl oz tomato juice

1 bay leaf

125 g/4½ oz cooked peeled small prawns

2 tomatoes, skinned, deseeded and chopped

½ tsp snipped fresh dill

salt and pepper

dill sprigs or fennel fronds, to garnish

1 Heat the olive oil in a large saucepan over a medium heat. Add the sliced onion and fennel and cook for 3–4 minutes, stirring occasionally, until the onion is just softened.

2 Add the potato, water, tomato juice and bay leaf with a large pinch of salt. Reduce the heat, cover and simmer for about 25 minutes, stirring once or twice, until the vegetables are soft.

3 Allow the soup to cool slightly, then transfer to a blender or food processor and purée until smooth, working in

batches if necessary. (If using a food processor, strain off the cooking liquid and reserve. Purée the soup solids with enough cooking liquid to moisten them, then combine with the remaining liquid.)

4 Return the soup to the saucepan and add the prawns. Simmer gently for about 10 minutes, to reheat the soup and allow it to absorb the prawn flavour.

5 Stir in the tomatoes and dill. Taste and adjust the seasoning, adding salt, if needed, and pepper. Thin the soup with a little more tomato juice, if wished. Ladle into warm bowls, garnish with dill sprigs or fennel fronds and serve.

Cullen Skink

This is a traditional, creamy Scottish soup. As the smoked haddock has quite a strong flavour, it has been mixed with some fresh cod.

NUTRITIONAL INFORMATION

Calories 108   Sugars 2.3g
Protein . . . . .7.4g   Fat 6.4g
Carbohydrate . . .5.6g   Saturates 3.9g

20 mins   40 mins

SERVES 4

INGREDIENTS

225 g/8 oz undyed smoked haddock fillet

2 tbsp butter

1 onion, finely chopped

600 ml/1 pint milk

350 g/12 oz potatoes, diced

350 g/12 oz cod, boned, skinned and cubed

150 ml/5 fl oz double cream

2 tbsp chopped fresh parsley

lemon juice, to taste

salt and pepper

TO GARNISH

lemon slices

parsley sprigs

1 Put the haddock fillet in a large frying pan and cover with boiling water. Leave for 10 minutes. Drain, reserving 300 ml/10 fl oz of the soaking water. Flake the fish, taking care to remove all the bones.

2 Heat the butter in a large saucepan and add the onion. Cook gently for 10 minutes until softened. Add the milk and bring to a gentle simmer before adding the potatoes. Cook for 10 minutes.

3 Add the reserved haddock flakes and cod. Simmer for an additional 10 minutes until the cod is tender.

4 Remove about one-third of the fish and potatoes, put in a food processor and blend until smooth. Alternatively, push through a sieve into a bowl. Return to the soup with the cream, parsley and seasoning. Taste and add a little lemon juice, if desired. Add a little of the reserved soaking water if the soup seems too thick. Reheat gently and serve the soup immediately.

COOK'S TIP

Look for Finnan haddock, if you can find it. Do not use yellow-dyed haddock fillet, which is often actually whiting and not haddock at all.

New England Clam Chowder

A chowder is a thick soup; the main ingredients are milk and potatoes, to which other flavours are added, such as fresh clams.

NUTRITIONAL INFORMATION

Calories	136	Sugars	.........2g
Protein	........7.7g	Fat	..........9.5g
Carbohydrate	...5.4g	Saturates	.....5.4g

15 mins   30 mins

SERVES 4

INGREDIENTS

900 g/2 lb live clams, reserving 8, in their shells, to garnish (see Cook's Tip)

4 rashers rindless streaky bacon, chopped

2 tbsp butter

1 onion, chopped

1 tbsp chopped fresh thyme

300 g/10½ oz potatoes, diced

300 ml/10 fl oz milk

1 bay leaf

150 ml/5 fl oz double cream

1 tbsp chopped fresh parsley

salt and pepper

1 Scrub the clams and put into a large saucepan with a splash of water. Cook over a high heat for 3–4 minutes until all the clams have opened. Discard any that remain closed. Strain the clams, reserving the cooking liquid. Set aside until cool enough to handle.

2 Remove the clams from their shells, roughly chop if large, and set aside.

3 In a clean saucepan, fry the bacon until browned and crisp. Drain on paper towels. Add the butter to the same pan and when it has melted, add the onion. Cook for 4–5 minutes until softened but not coloured. Add the thyme and cook briefly before adding the diced potatoes, reserved clam cooking liquid, milk and bay leaf. Bring to a boil and simmer for 10 minutes until the potatoes are tender but not falling apart. Remove the bay leaf.

4 Transfer to a food processor and blend until smooth or push through a sieve into a bowl.

5 Add the reserved clams, the bacon and the cream. Simmer for an additional 2–3 minutes until heated through. Season, then stir in the chopped parsley and serve.

COOK'S TIP

For a smart presentation, reserve 8 clams in their shells. Sit 2 on top of each bowl of soup to serve.

Creamy Scallop Soup

This delicately flavoured soup should not be overcooked. A sprinkling of parsley makes a pretty contrast to the creamy colour of the soup.

NUTRITIONAL INFORMATION

Calories 98   Sugars 1.4g
Protein . . . . .6.5g   Fat 5.6g
Carbohydrate . . .5.9g   Saturates 3.2g

10 mins   35 mins

SERVES 4

INGREDIENTS

4 tbsp butter

1 onion, finely chopped

450 g/1 lb potatoes, diced

600 ml/1 pint hot fish stock

350 g/12 oz prepared scallops, including corals if available

300 ml/10 fl oz milk

2 egg yolks

6 tbsp double cream

salt and pepper

1 tbsp chopped fresh parsley, to garnish

1 Melt the butter in a large saucepan over a gentle heat. Add the onion and cook very gently for 10 minutes until the onion is softened but not coloured. Add the potatoes and seasoning, cover and cook for an additional 10 minutes over a very low heat.

2 Pour on the hot fish stock, bring to the boil and simmer for an additional 10–15 minutes until the potatoes are tender.

3 Meanwhile, prepare the scallops. If the corals are available, roughly chop and set aside. Roughly chop the white meat and put in a second saucepan with the milk. Bring to a gentle simmer and cook for 6–8 minutes until the scallops are just tender.

4 When the potatoes are cooked, transfer them and their cooking liquid to a food processor or blender and blend to a purée. Alternatively, press through a nylon sieve. Return the mixture to a clean saucepan with the scallops and their milk and the pieces of coral, if using.

5 Whisk together the egg yolks and cream and add to the soup, off the heat. Return the soup to a very gentle heat and, stirring constantly, reheat the soup until it thickens slightly. Do not boil or the soup will curdle. Adjust seasoning and serve immediately, sprinkled with fresh parsley.

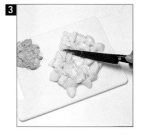

COOK'S TIP

The soup can be made in advance up to the point where the cream and eggs are added. They should only be added just before serving.

Pistou

This hearty soup of beans and vegetables is from Nice and gets its name from the fresh basil sauce stirred in at the last minute.

NUTRITIONAL INFORMATION

Calories ....55 Sugars 1.2g
Protein ....3.8g Fat 2.6g
Carbohydrate ...4.2g Saturates 0.6g

10 mins   25 mins

SERVES 6

INGREDIENTS

2 young carrots

450 g/1 lb potatoes

200 g/7 oz fresh peas in their shells

200 g/7 oz thin green beans

150 g/5½ oz young courgettes

2 tbsp olive oil

1 garlic clove, crushed

1 large onion, finely chopped

2.5 litres/4½ pints vegetable stock or water

1 bouquet garni of 2 sprigs fresh parsley
   and 1 bay leaf tied in a 7.5-cm/3-inch
   piece of celery

85 g/3 oz dried small soup pasta

1 large tomato, skinned, deseeded and
   chopped or diced

pared Parmesan cheese, to serve

PISTOU SAUCE

75 g/2¾ oz fresh basil leaves

1 garlic clove

5 tbsp fruity extra-virgin olive oil

salt and pepper

1 To make the pistou sauce, put the basil leaves, garlic and olive oil in a food processor and process until well blended. Season with salt and pepper to taste. Transfer to a bowl, cover with clingfilm and chill until required.

2 Peel the carrots and cut them in half lengthways, then slice. Peel the potatoes and cut into quarters lengthways, then slice. Set aside in a bowl of water until ready to use, to prevent discoloration.

3 Shell the peas. Top and tail the beans and cut them into 2.5-cm/1-inch pieces. Cut the courgettes in half lengthways, then slice.

4 Heat the oil in a large saucepan or flameproof casserole. Add the garlic and fry for 2 minutes, stirring. Add the onion and continue frying for 2 minutes until soft. Add the carrots and potatoes and stir for about 30 seconds.

5 Pour in the stock and bring to the boil. Lower the heat, partially cover and simmer for 8 minutes, until the vegetables are starting to become tender.

6 Stir in the peas, beans, courgettes, bouquet garni and pasta. Season and cook for 4 minutes, or until the vegetables and pasta are tender. Stir in the pistou sauce and serve with Parmesan.

Spinach & Ginger Soup

This mildly spiced, rich green soup is delicately scented with ginger and lemon grass. It makes a good light starter or summer lunch dish.

NUTRITIONAL INFORMATION

Calories	38	Sugars	.......0.8g
Protein	........3.2g	Fat	..........1.8g
Carbohydrate	...2.4g	Saturates	.....0.2g

5–10 mins   25 mins

SERVES 4

INGREDIENTS

2 tbsp sunflower oil

1 onion, chopped

2 garlic cloves, finely chopped

2 tsp fresh root ginger, finely chopped

250 g/9 oz fresh young spinach leaves

1 small lemon grass stalk, finely chopped

1 litre/1¾ pints chicken or vegetable stock

225 g/8 oz potatoes, chopped

1 tbsp rice wine or dry sherry

1 tsp sesame oil

salt and pepper

fresh spinach, finely shredded, to garnish

1 Heat the oil in a large saucepan. Add the onion, garlic and ginger, and fry gently for 3–4 minutes until softened but not browned.

2 Reserve 2–3 small spinach leaves. Add the remaining leaves and lemon grass to the saucepan, stirring until the spinach is wilted. Add the stock and potatoes to the pan and bring to the boil. Lower the heat, cover and simmer for about 10 minutes.

3 Tip the soup into a blender or food processor and process until completely smooth.

4 Return the soup to the pan and add the rice wine, then adjust the seasoning to taste with salt and pepper. Heat until just about to boil.

5 Finely shred the 2–3 reserved spinach leaves and scatter some over the top. Drizzle with a few drops of sesame oil and serve hot, garnished with the finely shredded fresh spinach leaves.

COOK'S TIP

To make a creamy-textured spinach and coconut soup, stir in about 4 tablespoons creamed coconut, or alternatively replace about 300 ml/10 fl oz of the stock with coconut milk. Serve the soup with shavings of fresh coconut scattered over the surface.

Bouillabaisse

This soup makes a festive seafood extravaganza worthy of any special occasion or celebration.

NUTRITIONAL INFORMATION

Calories 55   Sugars 1.1g
Protein ....7.2g   Fat 1.8g
Carbohydrate ...2.6g   Saturates 0.3g

 10 mins   1 hr 5 mins

SERVES 6

I N G R E D I E N T S

450 g/1 lb jumbo prawns

750 g/1 lb 10 oz firm white fish fillets, such as sea bass, snapper and monkfish

4 tbsp olive oil

grated rind of 1 orange

1 large garlic clove, finely chopped

½ tsp chilli paste or harissa

1 large leek, sliced

1 onion, halved and sliced

1 red pepper, cored, deseeded and sliced

3–4 tomatoes, cored and cut into eighths

4 garlic cloves, sliced

1 bay leaf

pinch of saffron threads

½ tsp fennel seeds

600 ml/1 pint water

1.2 litres/2 pints fish stock

1 fennel bulb, finely chopped

1 large onion, finely chopped

225 g/8 oz potatoes, halved and thinly sliced

250 g/9 oz scallops

salt and pepper

toasted French bread slices, to serve

ready-prepared aïoli, to serve

1 Peel the prawns and reserve the shells. Cut the fish fillets into serving pieces about 5 cm/2 inches square. Trim off any ragged edges and reserve. Put the fish in a bowl with 2 tablespoons of the olive oil, the orange rind, garlic and chilli paste or harissa. Turn to coat well, cover and chill the prawns and fish separately.

2 Heat 1 tablespoon of the olive oil in a large saucepan over a medium heat. Add the leek, sliced onion and red pepper. Cover and cook for 5 minutes, stirring, until the onion softens. Stir in the tomatoes, sliced garlic, bay leaf, saffron, fennel seeds, prawn shells, water and fish stock. Bring to the boil, then simmer, covered, for 30 minutes. Strain the stock.

3 Heat the remaining oil in a large pan. Add the fennel and chopped onion and cook for 5 minutes, stirring, until softened. Add the stock and potatoes and bring to the boil. Reduce the heat slightly, cover and cook for 12–15 minutes, until just tender.

4 Lower the heat and add the chilled fish, starting with thick pieces and adding thinner ones after 2–3 minutes. Add the chilled prawns and scallops and continue simmering gently until all the seafood is cooked and opaque throughout.

5 Taste the soup and adjust the seasoning. Ladle into warm bowls. Spread the aïoli sauce on the toasted bread slices and arrange on top of the soup.

Chicken & Vegetable Soup

This creamy soup is filled with chunky vegetables and aromatic herbs. Using baby vegetables gives the soup an attractive look.

NUTRITIONAL INFORMATION

Calories 77	Sugars 1.5g	
Protein 5.5g	Fats 3.3g	
Carbohydrates . .6.9g	Saturates 1.9g	

 5 mins   1 hr

SERVES 4

INGREDIENTS

1 litre/1¾ pints chicken stock

175 g/6 oz skinless boned chicken breast

fresh parsley and tarragon sprigs

2 garlic cloves, crushed

125 g/4½ oz baby carrots, halved or quartered

225 g/8 oz small new potatoes, quartered

4 tbsp plain flour

125 ml/4 fl oz milk

4–5 spring onions, sliced diagonally

85 g/3 oz asparagus tips, halved and cut into 4-cm/1½-inch pieces

125 ml/4 fl oz whipping or double cream

1 tbsp finely chopped fresh parsley

1 tbsp finely chopped fresh tarragon

salt and pepper

1 Put the stock in a saucepan with the chicken, parsley and tarragon sprigs and garlic. Bring just to the boil, reduce the heat, cover and simmer for 20 minutes, or until the chicken is cooked through and firm to the touch.

2 Remove the chicken and strain the stock. When the chicken is cool enough to handle, cut into bite-sized pieces.

3 Return the stock to the saucepan and bring to the boil. Adjust the heat so the liquid boils very gently. Add the carrots, cover and cook for 5 minutes. Add the potatoes, cover again and cook for about 12 minutes, or until the vegetables are beginning to become tender.

4 Meanwhile, put the flour in a small mixing bowl and very slowly whisk in the milk to make a thick paste. Pour in a little of the hot stock mixture and stir well to make a smooth liquid.

5 Stir the flour mixture into the soup and bring just to the boil, stirring. Boil gently for 4–5 minutes until it thickens, stirring frequently.

6 Add the spring onions, asparagus and chicken. Reduce the heat a little and simmer for about 15 minutes, until all the vegetables are tender. Stir in the cream and herbs. Season and serve.

Leek, Potato & Bacon Soup

Leek and potato soup is a classic recipe. Here the soup is enhanced with smoked bacon pieces and enriched with double cream for a little luxury.

NUTRITIONAL INFORMATION

Calories 93	Sugars 1g
Protein 3.3g	Fat 7.8g
Carbohydrate . . .2.7g	Saturates 4.4g

5 mins   30 mins

SERVES 4

INGREDIENTS

2 tbsp butter

175 g/6 oz potatoes, diced

4 leeks, shredded

2 garlic cloves, crushed

100 g/3½ oz smoked bacon, diced

850 ml/1½ pints vegetable stock

225 ml/8 fl oz double cream

2 tbsp chopped fresh parsley

salt and pepper

TO GARNISH

vegetable oil

1 leek, shredded

1 Melt the butter in a large saucepan and add the potatoes, leeks, garlic and bacon. Sauté gently for 5 minutes, stirring constantly.

2 Add the vegetable stock and bring to the boil. Reduce the heat, cover the saucepan and simmer for 20 minutes until the potatoes are cooked. Stir in the double cream and mix well.

3 Meanwhile, make the garnish. Half-fill a pan with oil and heat to 180°C–190°C/ 350°F–375°F or until a cube of bread browns in 30 seconds. Add the shredded leek and deep-fry for 1 minute until browned and crisp, taking care because it contains water. Drain the shredded leek thoroughly on paper towels and reserve.

4 Reserve a few pieces of potato, leek and bacon and set aside. Put the rest of the soup in a food processor or blender in batches and process each batch for 30 seconds. Return the puréed soup to a clean saucepan and heat through.

5 Stir in the reserved vegetables, bacon and parsley and season to taste. Pour into warmed bowls and garnish with the fried leeks.

VARIATION

For a lighter soup, omit the cream and stir yogurt or crème fraîche into the soup at the end of the cooking time.

Potato & Chorizo Soup

Chorizo is a spicy sausage originating from Spain where it is used to add its unique strong flavour to enhance many traditional dishes.

NUTRITIONAL INFORMATION

Calories	.55	Sugars	.1.2g
Protein	.3g	Fat	.1.6g
Carbohydrate	...7.8g	Saturates	....0.3g

5 mins   35 mins

SERVES 4

INGREDIENTS

2 tbsp olive oil

900 g/2 lb potatoes, cubed

2 red onions, quartered

1 garlic clove, crushed

1 litre/1¾ pints pork or vegetable stock

150 g/5½ oz Savoy cabbage, shredded

50 g/1¾ oz chorizo sausage, sliced

salt and pepper

paprika, to garnish

1 Heat the olive oil in a large saucepan and add the potatoes, red onions and garlic. Sauté gently for 5 minutes, stirring constantly, until softened.

2 Add the pork or vegetable stock and bring to the boil. Reduce the heat and cover the saucepan. Simmer the vegetables for about 20 minutes until the potatoes are tender.

3 Process the soup in a food processor or blender in 2 batches for 1 minute each. Return the puréed soup to a clean pan.

4 Add the shredded Savoy cabbage and chorizo sausage to the pan and cook for a further 7 minutes, stirring occasionally. Season with salt and pepper to taste.

5 Ladle the soup into warmed soup bowls, then garnish with a sprinkling of paprika and serve.

COOK'S TIP

Chorizo sausage requires no pre-cooking. In this recipe, it is added towards the end of the cooking time so that it does not overpower the other flavours in the soup.

Lentil, Potato & Ham Soup

A comforting and satisfying cold-weather soup, this is good served with bread as a light main course, but it is not too filling to be a starter soup.

NUTRITIONAL INFORMATION

Calories	61	Sugars	.......1.4g
Protein	........5.4g	Fat	..........0.8g
Carbohydrate	...8.6g	Saturates	.....0.3g

5 mins   45 mins

SERVES 4

I N G R E D I E N T S

300 g/10½ oz Puy lentils

2 tsp butter

1 large onion, finely chopped

2 carrots, finely chopped

1 garlic clove, finely chopped

450 ml/16 fl oz water

1 bay leaf

¼ tsp dried sage or rosemary

1 litre/1¾ pints chicken stock

225 g/8 oz potatoes, diced (see Cook's Tip)

1 tbsp tomato purée

115 g/4 oz smoked ham, finely diced

salt and pepper

chopped fresh parsley, to garnish

1 Rinse and drain the lentils and remove any small stones if necessary.

2 Melt the butter in a large saucepan or flameproof casserole over a medium heat. Add the onion, carrots and garlic, cover and cook for 4–5 minutes until the onion is slightly softened, stirring frequently.

3 Add the lentils to the vegetables with the water, bay leaf and sage or rosemary. Bring to the boil, reduce the heat, cover and simmer for 10 minutes.

4 Add the stock, potatoes, tomato purée and ham. Bring back to a simmer. Cover and continue simmering for 25–30 minutes, or until the vegetables are tender.

5 Season to taste with salt and pepper and remove the bay leaf. Ladle into warm bowls, garnish with parsley and serve.

COOK'S TIP

Cut the potatoes into small cubes, about 5 mm/¼ inch, so that they will be in proportion with the lentils.

Chinese Potato & Pork Broth

In this recipe the pork is seasoned with traditional Chinese flavourings – soy sauce, rice wine vinegar and a dash of sesame oil.

NUTRITIONAL INFORMATION

Calories ....166 Sugars 2g
Protein ....10g Fat 5g
Carbohydrate ...26g Saturates 1g

🍲 5 mins   🕐 20 mins

SERVES 4

I N G R E D I E N T S

1 litre/1¾ pints chicken stock

600 g/1 lb 5 oz potatoes, diced

2 tbsp rice wine vinegar

2 tbsp cornflour

4 tbsp water

125 g/4½ oz pork fillet, sliced

1 tbsp light soy sauce

1 tsp sesame oil

1 carrot, cut into matchsticks

1 tsp fresh root ginger, chopped

3 spring onions, sliced thinly

1 red pepper, sliced

225 g/8 oz canned bamboo shoots, drained

VARIATION

For extra heat, add 1 chopped red chilli or 1 teaspoon of chilli powder to the soup in step 5.

1 Add the chicken stock, potatoes and 1 tablespoon of the rice wine vinegar to a saucepan and bring to the boil. Reduce the heat until the stock is just simmering.

2 Mix the cornflour with the water then stir into the hot stock.

3 Bring the stock back to the boil, stirring until thickened, then reduce the heat until it is just simmering again.

4 Place the pork slices in a dish and season with the remaining rice wine vinegar, the soy sauce and sesame oil.

5 Add the pork slices, carrot matchsticks and ginger to the stock and cook for 10 minutes. Stir in the spring onions, red pepper and bamboo shoots. Cook for a further 5 minutes. Pour the soup into warmed bowls and serve immediately.

Chunky Potato & Beef Soup

This is a real winter warmer – pieces of tender beef and chunky mixed vegetables are cooked in a liquor flavoured with sherry.

NUTRITIONAL INFORMATION

Calories	187	Sugars	.........3g
Protein	........14g	Fat	...........9g
Carbohydrate	...12g	Saturates	......2g

 5 mins   35 mins

SERVES 4

INGREDIENTS

2 tbsp vegetable oil

225 g/8 oz lean braising or frying steak, cut into strips

225 g/8 oz new potatoes, halved

1 carrot, diced

2 celery sticks, sliced

2 leeks, sliced

850 ml/1½ pints beef stock

8 baby sweetcorn cobs, sliced

1 bouquet garni

2 tbsp dry sherry

salt and pepper

chopped fresh parsley, to garnish

1 Heat the vegetable oil in a large saucepan.

2 Add the strips of meat to the saucepan and cook for 3 minutes, turning constantly.

3 Add the potatoes, carrot, celery and leeks. Cook for a further 5 minutes, stirring frequently.

4 Pour the beef stock into the saucepan and bring to the boil. Reduce the heat until the liquid is simmering, then add the sliced baby sweetcorn cobs and the bouquet garni.

5 Cook the soup for a further 20 minutes or until cooked through.

6 Remove the bouquet garni from the saucepan and discard. Stir the dry sherry into the soup and then season to taste with salt and pepper.

7 Pour the soup into warmed bowls and garnish with the chopped fresh parsley. Serve at once with crusty bread.

COOK'S TIP

Make double the quantity of soup and freeze the remainder in a rigid container for later use. When ready to use, leave in the refrigerator to defrost thoroughly, then heat until piping hot.

Indian Bean Soup

A thick and hearty soup, nourishing and substantial enough to serve as a main meal with wholemeal bread.

NUTRITIONAL INFORMATION

Calories 237	Sugars 9g
Protein 9g	Fat 9g
Carbohydrate . . .33g	Saturates 1g

🥗 20 mins   🕐 50 mins

SERVES 6

I N G R E D I E N T S

4 tbsp vegetable ghee or vegetable oil

2 onions, peeled and chopped

225 g/8 oz potato, cut into chunks

225 g/8 oz parsnip, cut into chunks

225 g/8 oz turnip or swede, cut into chunks

2 celery sticks, sliced

2 courgettes, sliced

1 green pepper, deseeded and cut into
    1 cm/½ inch pieces

2 garlic cloves, crushed

2 tsp ground coriander

1 tbsp paprika

1 tbsp mild curry paste

1.2 litres/2 pints vegetable stock

salt

400 g/14 oz canned black-eye beans,
    drained and rinsed

chopped coriander, to garnish (optional)

1 Heat the ghee or oil in a saucepan, add all the prepared vegetables, except the courgettes and green pepper, and cook over a moderate heat, stirring frequently, for 5 minutes. Add the garlic, ground coriander, paprika and curry paste and cook, stirring constantly, for 1 minute.

2 Stir in the stock and season with salt to taste. Bring to the boil, cover and simmer over a low heat, stirring occasionally, for 25 minutes.

3 Stir in the black-eye beans, sliced courgettes and green pepper, then replace the lid and continue cooking for a further 15 minutes, or until all the vegetables are tender.

4 Process 300 ml/10 fl oz of the soup mixture (about 2 ladlefuls) in a food processor or blender. Return the puréed mixture to the soup in the saucepan and reheat until piping hot. Sprinkle with chopped coriander if using, and serve hot.

Potato Skins & Two Fillings

Potato skins are always a favourite. Prepare the skins in advance and warm them through before serving with the salad fillings.

NUTRITIONAL INFORMATION

Calories 279	Sugars 2g	
Protein 5g	Fats 11g	
Carbohydrate ...44g	Saturates 7g	

30 mins   1 hr 10 mins

SERVES 4

INGREDIENTS

4 large baking potatoes

2 tbsp vegetable oil

4 tsp salt

150 ml/5 fl oz soured cream and 2 tbsp chopped chives, to serve

snipped chives, to garnish

BEANSPROUT SALAD

50 g/1¾ oz beansprouts

1 celery stick, sliced

1 orange, peeled and segmented

1 red eating apple, chopped

½ red pepper, deseeded and chopped

1 tbsp chopped parsley

1 tbsp light soy sauce

1 tbsp clear honey

1 small garlic clove, crushed

BEAN FILLING

100 g/3½ oz canned, mixed beans, drained

1 onion, halved and sliced

1 tomato, chopped

2 spring onions, chopped

2 tsp lemon juice

salt and pepper

1 Scrub the potatoes and put on a baking tray. Prick the potatoes all over with a fork and rub the oil and salt into the skin.

2 Cook in a preheated oven at 200°C/400°F/Gas Mark 6 for 1 hour or until soft.

3 Cut the potatoes in half lengthwise and scoop out the flesh, leaving a 1-cm/½-inch thick shell. Put the shells, skin side uppermost, in the oven for 10 minutes until crisp.

4 Mix the ingredients for the beansprout salad in a bowl, tossing in the soy sauce, honey and garlic to coat.

5 Mix all the ingredients for the bean filling together in a separate bowl.

6 In another bowl, mix together the soured cream and chives until well combined.

7 Serve the potato skins hot, with the two salad fillings, garnished with snipped chives, and the soured cream and chive sauce.

Carrot & Potato Medley

This is a colourful dish of shredded vegetables in a fresh garlic and honey dressing. It is delicious served with crusty bread to mop up the dressing.

NUTRITIONAL INFORMATION

Calories 81   Sugars 4.1g
Protein . . . . .1g   Fat 5.6g
Carbohydrate . . . .7g   Saturates 0.8g

 5 mins   🕐 5 mins

SERVES 4

I N G R E D I E N T S

2 tbsp olive oil

225 g/8 oz potatoes, cut into thin strips

1 fennel bulb, cut into thin strips

2 carrots, grated

1 red onion, cut into thin strips

chopped chives and fennel fronds,
    to garnish

D R E S S I N G

3 tbsp olive oil

1 tbsp garlic wine vinegar

1 garlic clove, crushed

1 tsp Dijon mustard

2 tsp clear honey

salt and pepper

1 Heat the olive oil in a frying pan, add the potato and fennel slices and cook for 2–3 minutes until beginning to brown. Remove from the pan with a slotted spoon and drain on kitchen paper.

2 Arrange the carrots, red onion and potatoes and fennel in separate piles on a serving plate.

3 Mix the dressing ingredients together and pour over the vegetables. Toss well and sprinkle with chopped chives and fennel fronds. Serve immediately or cool and leave in the refrigerator until required.

VARIATION
Use mixed, grilled peppers or shredded leeks in this dish for variety, or add beansprouts and a segmented orange, if you prefer.

Mixed Bean & Apple Salad

Use any mixture of beans you have to hand in this recipe, but the wider the variety, the more colourful the salad.

NUTRITIONAL INFORMATION

Calories 183   Sugars 8g
Protein ....6g   Fat 7g
Carbohydrate ...26g   Saturates 1g

20 mins   20 mins

SERVES 4

INGREDIENTS

225 g/8 oz new potatoes, scrubbed and quartered

225 g/8 oz mixed canned beans, such as red kidney beans, flageolet and borlotti beans, drained and rinsed

1 red eating apple, diced and tossed in 1 tbsp lemon juice

1 yellow pepper, deseeded and diced

1 shallot, sliced

½ fennel bulb, sliced

oak-leaf lettuce leaves

DRESSING

1 tbsp red wine vinegar

2 tbsp olive oil

½ tbsp American mustard

1 garlic clove, crushed

2 tsp chopped fresh thyme

VARIATION

Use Dijon or wholegrain mustard in place of American mustard for a different flavour.

1 Cook the quartered potatoes in a saucepan of boiling water for 15 minutes, until tender. Drain and transfer to a mixing bowl.

2 Add the mixed beans to the potatoes, together with the apple, pepper, shallot and fennel. Mix well, taking care not to break up the cooked potatoes.

3 To make the dressing, whisk all the dressing ingredients together until thoroughly combined, then pour it over the potato salad.

4 Line a serving plate or salad bowl with the oak-leaf lettuce leaves and spoon the potato mixture into the centre. Serve the salad immediately.

Beetroot Salad & Dill Dressing

The beetroot adds a rich colour to this dish. The dill dressing with the potatoes is a classic combination.

NUTRITIONAL INFORMATION

Calories	174	Sugars	.........8g
Protein	.........4g	Fat	...........6g
Carbohydrate	...27g	Saturates	......1g

 25 mins   15 mins

SERVES 4

INGREDIENTS

450 g/1 lb waxy potatoes, diced

4 small cooked beetroot, sliced

½ small cucumber, thinly sliced

2 large dill pickles, sliced

1 red onion, halved and sliced

dill sprigs, to garnish

DRESSING

1 garlic clove, crushed

2 tbsp olive oil

2 tbsp red wine vinegar

2 tbsp chopped fresh dill

salt and pepper

COOK'S TIP

If making the salad in advance, do not mix the beetroot and potatoes until just before serving, because the beetroot will bleed its colour.

1 Cook the potatoes in a saucepan of boiling water for 15 minutes or until tender. Drain and leave to cool.

2 When cool, mix the potatoes and beetroots together in a bowl, cover with clingfilm and set aside.

3 Line a salad platter with the slices of cucumber, dill pickles and red onion.

4 Spoon the potato and beetroot mixture into the centre of the platter.

5 In a small bowl, whisk all the dressing ingredients together, then pour the dressing over the salad.

6 Serve the potato and beetroot salad immediately (see Cook's Tip, left), garnished with dill sprigs.

Radish & Cucumber Salad

The radishes and the herb and mustard dressing give this colourful salad a mild mustard flavour that complements the potatoes perfectly.

NUTRITIONAL INFORMATION

Calories 140	Sugars 3g	
Protein 3g	Fat 6g	
Carbohydrate ...20g	Saturates 1g	

 50 mins   20 mins

SERVES 4

INGREDIENTS

500 g/1 lb 2 oz new potatoes, scrubbed and halved

½ cucumber, thinly sliced

2 tsp salt

1 bunch radishes, thinly sliced

DRESSING

1 tbsp Dijon mustard

2 tbsp olive oil

1 tbsp white wine vinegar

2 tbsp mixed chopped herbs

1 Cook the potatoes in a saucepan of boiling water for 10–15 minutes, or until tender. Drain and set aside to cool.

2 Meanwhile, spread out the cucumber slices on a plate and sprinkle with the salt. Leave to stand for 30 minutes, then rinse under cold running water and pat dry with kitchen paper.

3 Arrange the cucumber and radish slices on a serving plate in a decorative pattern and pile the cooked potatoes in the centre of the slices.

4 In a small bowl, mix all the dressing ingredients together, whisking until thoroughly combined. Pour the dressing over the salad, tossing well to coat all of the ingredients. Chill in the refrigerator before serving.

COOK'S TIP

The cucumber adds not only colour but also a real freshness to the salad. It is salted and left to stand to remove the excess water, which would make the salad soggy. Wash the cucumber well to remove all of the salt before adding to the salad.

Sweet Potato Salad

This hot fruity salad combines sweet potato and fried bananas with colourful mixed peppers, tossed in a honey-based dressing.

NUTRITIONAL INFORMATION

Calories 424   Sugars 29g
Protein . . . . .5g   Fat 17g
Carbohydrate . . .68g   Saturates 8g

 15 mins   20 mins

SERVES 4

I N G R E D I E N T S

500 g/1 lb 2 oz sweet potatoes, diced

4 tbsp butter

1 tbsp lemon juice

1 garlic clove, crushed

1 red pepper, deseeded and diced

1 green pepper, deseeded and diced

2 bananas, thickly sliced

2 thick slices white bread, crusts removed, diced

salt and pepper

D R E S S I N G

2 tbsp clear honey

2 tbsp chopped chives

2 tbsp lemon juice

2 tbsp olive oil

1 Cook the sweet potatoes in a saucepan of boiling water for 10–15 minutes, until tender. Drain thoroughly and reserve.

2 Meanwhile, melt the butter in a frying pan. Add the lemon juice, garlic and peppers and cook, stirring constantly for 3 minutes.

3 Add the banana slices to the pan and cook for 1 minute. Remove the bananas from the pan with a slotted spoon and stir into the potatoes.

4 Add the bread cubes to the frying pan and cook, stirring frequently, for 2 minutes, until they are golden brown on all sides.

5 Mix the dressing ingredients together in a small saucepan and heat until the honey is runny.

6 Spoon the potato mixture into a serving dish and season to taste with salt and pepper. Pour the dressing over the potatoes and sprinkle the croûtons over the top. Serve immediately.

COOK'S TIP

Use firm, slightly underripe bananas in this recipe because they won't turn soft and mushy when they are fried.

Sweet Potato & Nut Salad

Pecan nuts with their slightly bitter flavour are mixed with sweet potatoes to make a sweet and sour salad with an interesting texture.

NUTRITIONAL INFORMATION

Calories ......330 Sugars 5g
Protein ....4g Fat 20g
Carbohydrate ...36g Saturates 2g

 25 mins   10 mins

SERVES 4

INGREDIENTS

500 g/1 lb 2 oz sweet potatoes, diced

2 celery sticks, sliced

125 g/4½ oz celeriac, grated

2 spring onions, sliced

50 g/1¾ oz pecan nuts, chopped

2 heads chicory, separated

1 tsp lemon juice

thyme sprigs, to garnish

DRESSING

4 tbsp vegetable oil

1 tbsp garlic wine vinegar

1 tsp soft light brown sugar

2 tsp chopped fresh thyme

1 Cook the sweet potatoes in a large saucepan of boiling water for 10–15 minutes, until tender. Drain thoroughly and set aside to cool.

2 When the potatoes have cooled, stir in the celery, celeriac, spring onions and pecan nuts.

3 Line a salad plate with the chicory leaves and sprinkle with lemon juice.

4 Spoon the sweet potato mixture into the centre of the leaves.

5 In a small bowl, whisk the dressing ingredients together.

6 Pour the dressing over the salad and serve at once, garnished with fresh thyme sprigs.

COOK'S TIP

Sweet potatoes do not store as well as ordinary potatoes. It is best to store them in a cool, dark place (not the refrigerator) and use within 1 week of purchase.

Indian Potato Salad

There are many hot, spicy, Indian potato dishes that are served with curry, but this fruity salad is delicious chilled.

NUTRITIONAL INFORMATION

Calories	175	Sugars	.........8g
Protein	.........6g	Fat	...........1g
Carbohydrate	...38g	Saturates	.....0.3g

25 mins   20 mins

SERVES 4

I N G R E D I E N T S

900 g/2 lb floury potatoes, diced

75 g/2¾ oz small broccoli florets

1 small mango, diced

4 spring onions, sliced

salt and pepper

small cooked spiced poppadoms, to serve

D R E S S I N G

½ tsp ground cumin

½ tsp ground coriander

1 tbsp mango chutney

150 ml/5 fl oz low-fat natural yogurt

1 tsp fresh root ginger, chopped

2 tbsp chopped fresh coriander

1 Cook the potatoes in a saucepan of boiling water for 10 minutes or until tender. Drain and place in a mixing bowl.

2 Meanwhile, blanch the broccoli florets in a separate saucepan of boiling water for 2 minutes. Drain the broccoli well and add the florets to the potatoes in the bowl.

3 When the potatoes and broccoli have cooled, add the mango and spring onions. Season to taste with salt and pepper and mix well to combine.

4 In a small bowl, stir all of the dressing ingredients together.

5 Spoon the dressing over the potato mixture and mix together carefully, taking care not to break up the potatoes and broccoli.

6 Serve the salad immediately, accompanied by the small cooked spiced poppadoms.

COOK'S TIP

Mix the dressing ingredients together in advance and leave to chill in the refrigerator for a few hours in order for a stronger flavour to develop.

Mexican Potato Salad

The flavours of Mexico are echoed in this dish where potato slices are topped with tomatoes and chillies, and served with guacamole.

NUTRITIONAL INFORMATION

Calories	260	Sugars	.........6g
Protein	.........6g	Fat	...........9g
Carbohydrate	...41g	Saturates	.......2g

20 mins   20 mins

SERVES 4

INGREDIENTS

1.25 kg/2 lb 12 oz waxy potatoes, sliced

1 ripe avocado

1 tsp olive oil

1 tsp lemon juice

1 garlic clove, crushed

1 onion, chopped

2 large tomatoes, sliced

1 green chilli, chopped

1 yellow pepper, deseeded and sliced

2 tbsp chopped fresh coriander

salt and pepper

lemon wedges, to garnish

1 Cook the potato slices in a saucepan of boiling water for 10–15 minutes, or until tender. Drain and set aside to cool.

2 Meanwhile, cut the avocado in half and remove the stone. Mash the avocado flesh with a fork (you could also scoop the avocado flesh from the 2 halves using a spoon and then mash it).

3 Add the olive oil, lemon juice, garlic and onion to the avocado flesh and stir to mix. Cover the bowl with clingfilm, to minimize discoloration, and set aside.

4 Mix the tomatoes, chilli and yellow pepper together and transfer to a salad bowl with the potato slices.

5 Arrange the avocado mixture on top of the salad and sprinkle with the chopped coriander. Season to taste with salt and pepper and serve garnished with lemon wedges.

VARIATION
You can omit the green chilli from this salad if you do not like hot dishes.

Nests of Chinese Salad

Crisp fried potato nests are perfect as an edible salad bowl and delicious when filled with a colourful Chinese-style salad of vegetables and fruit.

NUTRITIONAL INFORMATION

Calories 272   Sugars 11g
Protein ....4g   Fat 4g
Carbohydrate ...59g   Saturates 0.4g

 15 mins   🕑 15 mins

SERVES 4

INGREDIENTS

POTATO NESTS

450 g/1 lb floury potatoes, grated

125 g/4½ oz cornflour

vegetable oil, for frying

fresh chives, to garnish

SALAD

125 g/4½ oz pineapple, cubed

1 green pepper, cut into strips

1 carrot, cut into matchsticks

50 g/1¾ oz mangetouts, thickly sliced

4 baby sweetcorn cobs, halved lengthways

25 g/1 oz beansprouts

2 spring onions, sliced

DRESSING

1 tbsp clear honey

1 tsp light soy sauce

1 garlic clove, crushed

1 tsp lemon juice

1 To make the nests, rinse the potatoes several times in cold water. Drain well on kitchen paper so that they are completely dry. This is to prevent the potatoes from spitting when they are cooked in the fat. Place the potatoes in a mixing bowl. Add the cornflour, mixing well to coat the potatoes.

2 Half fill a wok with vegetable oil and heat until smoking. Line a 15-cm/6-inch diameter wire sieve with a quarter of the potato mixture and press another sieve of the same size on top.

3 Lower the sieves into the oil and cook for 2 minutes until the potato nest is golden brown and crisp. Remove from the wok, allowing the excess oil to drain off.

4 Repeat 3 more times to use up all of the mixture and make a total of 4 nests. Leave to cool.

5 Mix the salad ingredients together, then spoon into the potato baskets.

6 To make the dressing, mix all of the dressing ingredients together. Pour the dressing over the salad, garnish with chives and serve immediately.

Potato, Rocket & Apple Salad

This green and white salad is made with creamy, salty-flavoured goat's cheese — its distinctive flavour is perfect with salad leaves.

NUTRITIONAL INFORMATION

Calories 104	Sugars 3.1g
Protein 3.1g	Fat 5.3g
Carbohydrate . .11.8g	Saturates 1.5g

5 mins, plus 15 mins cooling time

15 mins

SERVES 4

I N G R E D I E N T S

600 g/1 lb 5 oz potatoes, unpeeled and sliced

2 green dessert apples, diced

1 tsp lemon juice

25 g/1 oz walnut pieces

125 g/4½ oz goat's cheese, cubed

150 g/5½ oz rocket leaves

salt and pepper

D R E S S I N G

2 tbsp olive oil

1 tbsp red wine vinegar

1 tsp clear honey

1 tsp fennel seeds

COOK'S TIP

Serve this salad immediately to prevent the apple from discolouring. Alternatively, prepare all of the other ingredients in advance and add the apple at the last minute.

1 Cook the potatoes in a pan of boiling water for 15 minutes until tender. Drain and leave to cool. Transfer the cooled potatoes to a serving bowl.

2 Toss the diced apples in the lemon juice, then drain and stir them into the cold potatoes.

3 Add the walnut pieces, cheese cubes and rocket leaves, then toss the ingredients together to mix.

4 In a small bowl, whisk all of the dressing ingredients together and then pour the dressing over the salad. Season to taste and serve immediately.

Light Meals & Side Dishes

Potatoes are very versatile and can be used as a base to create an array of tempting light meals and satisfying snacks. They are also nutritious, and their carbohydrate gives a welcome energy boost. As potatoes have a fairly neutral flavour, they can be teamed with a variety of other ingredients and flavours.

This chapter contains a range of delicious yet light meals – try Feta & Spinach Omelette, or Soured Cream & Salmon Pancakes. Potatoes can be cooked in a variety of ways, such as mashing, roasting, deep-frying and baking, making them an adaptable and valuable component of any meal.

Potatoes with a Spicy Filling

Crisp, twice-baked potatoes are partnered with an unusual filling of the Middle Eastern flavours of chickpeas, cumin and coriander.

NUTRITIONAL INFORMATION

Calories 335	Sugars 7g
Protein 15g	Fat 7g
Carbohydrate . . .57g	Saturates 1g

 20 mins   1 hr 30 mins

SERVES 4

I N G R E D I E N T S

4 large baking potatoes

1 tbsp vegetable oil, optional

430 g/15½ oz canned chickpeas, drained

1 tsp ground coriander

1 tsp ground cumin

4 tbsp chopped fresh coriander

150 ml/5 fl oz low-fat natural yogurt

salt and pepper

S A L A D

2 tomatoes

4 tbsp chopped fresh coriander

½ cucumber

½ red onion

1 Preheat the oven to 200°C/400°F/Gas Mark 6.

2 Scrub the potatoes and pat them dry with absorbent kitchen paper. Prick them all over with a fork, brush with oil (if using) and season with salt and pepper.

COOK'S TIP

For an even lower fat version of this recipe, bake the potatoes without oiling them first.

3 Place the potatoes on a baking tray and bake for 1–1¼ hours or until cooked through. Cool for 10 minutes.

4 Meanwhile, put the chickpeas in a large bowl and mash with a fork or potato masher. Stir in the ground coriander, cumin and half the fresh coriander. Cover with clingfilm and set aside.

5 Halve the cooked potatoes and scoop the flesh into a bowl, keeping the shells intact. Mash the flesh until smooth and gently mix into the chickpea mixture with the natural yogurt. Season to taste.

6 Place the potato shells on a baking tray and fill with the potato and chickpea mixture. Return the potatoes to the oven and bake for 10–15 minutes until heated through.

7 Meanwhile, make the salad. Using a sharp knife, chop the tomatoes. Slice the cucumber and cut the red onion into thin slices. Toss all the ingredients together in a serving dish.

8 Serve the potatoes sprinkled with the remaining chopped coriander and the prepared salad.

Vegetable Samosas

These Indian snacks are perfect for a quick or light meal, served with a salad. They can be made and frozen in advance for ease of use.

NUTRITIONAL INFORMATION

Calories 291	Sugars 2g	
Protein 4g	Fat 23g	
Carbohydrate . . .18g	Saturates 3g	

20 mins   30 mins

MAKES 12

INGREDIENTS

FILLING

2 tbsp vegetable oil

1 onion, chopped

½ tsp ground coriander

½ tsp ground cumin

pinch of turmeric

½ tsp ground ginger

½ tsp garam masala

1 garlic clove, crushed

225 g/8 oz potatoes, diced

100 g/3½ oz frozen peas, thawed

150 g/5½ oz spinach, chopped

PASTRY

350 g/12 oz (12 sheets) filo pastry

oil, for deep-frying

1 To make the filling, heat the oil in a frying pan. Add the onion and sauté, stirring frequently, for 1–2 minutes, until softened. Stir in all of the spices and garlic and cook for 1 minute.

2 Add the potatoes and cook over a low heat, stirring frequently, for 5 minutes, until they begin to soften.

3 Stir in the peas and spinach and cook for a further 3–4 minutes.

4 Lay the filo pastry sheets out on a clean work surface and fold each sheet in half lengthways.

5 Place 2 tablespoons of the vegetable filling at one end of each folded pastry sheet. Fold over one corner to make a triangle. Continue folding in this way to make a triangular package and seal the edges with water.

6 Repeat with the remaining pastry and the remaining filling.

7 Heat the oil for deep-frying to 180°C/350°F or until a cube of bread browns in 30 seconds. Fry the samosas, in batches, for 1–2 minutes until golden. Drain on absorbent kitchen paper and keep warm while cooking the remainder. Serve immediately.

Gnocchi with Tomato Sauce

These gnocchi, or small dumplings, are made with potato, flavoured with spinach and nutmeg and served in a delicious tomato and basil sauce.

NUTRITIONAL INFORMATION

Calories 337   Sugars 4g
Protein . . . . .9g   Fat 10g
Carbohydrate . . .52g   Saturates 4g

 25 mins   1 hr

SERVES 4

I N G R E D I E N T S

450 g/1 lb baking potatoes

75 g/2¾ oz spinach

1 tsp water

3 tbsp butter or margarine

1 small egg, beaten

150 g/5½ oz plain flour

fresh basil leaves, to garnish

T O M A T O   S A U C E

1 tbsp olive oil

1 shallot, chopped

1 tbsp tomato purée

225 g/8 oz canned chopped tomatoes

2 tbsp chopped fresh basil

6 tbsp red wine

1 tsp caster sugar

salt and pepper

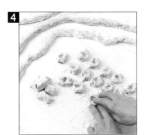

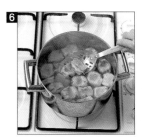

1 Cook the potatoes in their skins in a pan of boiling salted water for 20 minutes. Drain well and press through a sieve into a bowl.

2 Cook the spinach in the water for 5 minutes or until wilted. Drain and pat dry with paper towels, then chop and stir into the potatoes.

3 Add the butter or margarine, egg and half of the flour to the spinach mixture, mixing well. Turn out on to a floured surface, gradually kneading in the remaining flour to form a soft dough.

4 With floured hands, roll the dough into thin ropes and cut off 2-cm/¾-inch pieces. Press the centre of each dumpling with your finger, drawing it towards you to curl the sides of the gnocchi. Cover the gnocchi with clingfilm and leave to chill.

5 Heat the oil for the sauce in a pan and sauté the chopped shallots for 5 minutes. Add the tomato purée, tomatoes, basil, red wine and sugar and season well. Bring to the boil and then simmer for 20 minutes.

6 Bring a pan of salted water to the boil and cook the gnocchi for 2–3 minutes or until they rise to the top of the pan. Drain well and transfer to serving dishes. Spoon the tomato sauce over the gnocchi. Garnish with basil and serve.

Vegetable Burgers & Chips

These spicy vegetable burgers are delicious, especially in a warm bun or roll and served with the light oven chips.

NUTRITIONAL INFORMATION

Calories . . . . .461 Sugars 4g

Protein . . . . .18g Fat 17g

Carbohydrate . . .64g Saturates 2g

 15 mins, plus 30 mins chilling time   1 hr

SERVES 4

I N G R E D I E N T S

VEGETABLE BURGERS

100 g/3½ oz spinach

2 tbsp olive oil

1 leek, chopped

2 garlic cloves, crushed

100 g/3½ oz mushrooms, chopped

300 g/10½ oz firm tofu, chopped

1 tsp chilli powder

1 tsp curry powder

1 tbsp chopped fresh coriander

75 g/2¾ oz fresh wholemeal breadcrumbs

burger bap or roll and salad, to serve

CHIPS

2 large potatoes

2 tbsp plain flour

1 tsp chilli powder

2 tbsp olive oil

1 To make the burgers, cook the spinach in a little boiling water for 2 minutes. Drain thoroughly and pat dry with kitchen paper.

2 Heat 1 tablespoon of the oil in a frying pan and sauté the leek and garlic for 2–3 minutes. Add the remaining ingredients, except the breadcrumbs, and cook for 5–7 minutes, until the vegetables have softened. Toss in the spinach and cook for 1 minute.

3 Transfer the mixture to a food processor and process for 30 seconds, until almost smooth. Transfer to a bowl, stir in the breadcrumbs, mixing well, and leave until cool enough to handle. Using floured hands, form the mixture into four equal-sized burgers. Leave to chill for 30 minutes.

4 To make the chips, cut the potatoes into thin wedges and cook in a pan of boiling water for 10 minutes. Drain and toss in the flour and chilli powder. Lay the chips on a baking tray and sprinkle with the oil. Cook in a preheated oven, 200°C/400°F/Gas Mark 6, for 30 minutes, or until golden.

5 Meanwhile, heat the remaining oil in a frying pan and cook the burgers for 8–10 minutes, turning once. Place in a bap, add some salad, and serve with the chips.

Puff Potato Pie

This pie with its rich filling is a great alternative to serving potatoes as a side dish with any meal. Alternatively, serve with salad for a light lunch.

NUTRITIONAL INFORMATION

Calories 198   Sugars 1.4g
Protein . . . . .3.7g   Fat 12.4g
Carbohydrate . .19.8g   Saturates 2.9g

   5–10 mins   50 mins, plus 20–30 mins cooling time

SERVES 6

INGREDIENTS

700 g/1 lb 9 oz potatoes, thinly sliced

2 spring onions, finely chopped

1 red onion, finely chopped

150 ml/5 fl oz double cream

500 g/1 lb 2 oz fresh ready-made puff pastry

2 eggs, beaten

salt and pepper

1 Lightly grease a baking tray. Bring a saucepan of water to the boil, add the sliced potatoes, bring back to the boil and then simmer for a few minutes. Drain the potato slices and leave to cool. Dry off any excess moisture with kitchen paper.

2 In a bowl, mix together the spring onions, red onion and the cooled potato slices. Stir in 2 tablespoons of the cream and plenty of seasoning.

3 Divide the pastry in half and roll out one piece to a 23-cm/9-inch round. Roll the remaining pastry to a 25-cm/10-inch round.

4 Place the smaller circle on to the baking tray and top with the potato mixture, leaving a 2.5-cm/1-inch border. Brush this border with a little of the beaten egg.

5 Top with the larger circle of pastry, seal well and crimp the edges of the pastry. Cut a steam vent in the middle of the pastry and, using the back of a knife, mark with a pattern. Brush with the beaten egg and bake in a preheated oven, 200°C/400°F/Gas Mark 6, for 30 minutes.

6 Mix the remaining beaten egg with the rest of the cream and pour into the pie through the steam vent. Return the pie to the oven for 15 minutes, then remove it and leave it to cool for 30 minutes. Serve warm or cold.

COOK'S TIP

The filling may be prepared up to 4 hours in advance.

Potato & Bean Pâté

This pâté is easy to prepare and may be stored in the refrigerator for up to two days. Serve with small toasts, Melba toast or crudités.

NUTRITIONAL INFORMATION

Calories 84   Sugars 3g
Protein ....5.1g   Fat 0.5g
Carbohydrate ..15.7g Saturates 0.1g

🥔 3 mins   🕐 10 mins

SERVES 4

I N G R E D I E N T S

100 g/3½ oz floury potatoes, diced

225 g/8 oz mixed canned beans, such as borlotti, flageolet and kidney beans, drained

1 garlic clove, crushed

2 tsp lime juice

1 tbsp chopped fresh coriander

2 tbsp natural yogurt

salt and pepper

chopped fresh coriander, to garnish

1 Cook the potatoes in a saucepan of boiling water for 10 minutes until tender. Drain well and mash.

2 Transfer the potato to a food processor or blender and add the beans, garlic, lime juice and the fresh coriander. Season the mixture and process for 1 minute to make a smooth purée. Alternatively, mix the beans with the potato, garlic, lime juice and coriander and mash well.

3 Turn the purée into a bowl and add the yogurt. Mix together thoroughly.

4 Spoon the pâté into a serving dish and garnish with the chopped coriander. Serve at once or cover with clingfilm and leave to chill before use.

COOK'S TIP

To make Melba toast, toast ready-sliced white or brown bread lightly on both sides under a preheated high grill and remove the crusts. Holding the bread flat, slide a sharp knife between the toasted bread to split it horizontally. Cut into triangles and toast the untoasted sides.

Mixed Mushroom Cakes

These cakes are packed with creamy potato and a variety of mushrooms and will be loved by vegetarians and meat-eaters alike.

NUTRITIONAL INFORMATION

Calories 298	Sugars 0.8g	
Protein 5g	Fat 22g	
Carbohydrate ...22g	Saturates 5g	

 20 mins   25 mins

SERVES 4

INGREDIENTS

500 g/1 lb 2 oz floury potatoes, diced

2 tbsp butter

175 g/6 oz mixed mushrooms, chopped

2 garlic cloves, crushed

1 small egg, beaten

1 tbsp chopped fresh chives, plus extra
   to garnish

flour, for dusting

oil, for frying

salt and pepper

1 Cook the potatoes in a pan of lightly salted boiling water for 10 minutes, or until cooked through.

2 Drain the potatoes well, mash with a potato masher or fork and set aside.

3 Meanwhile, melt the butter in a frying pan. Add the mushrooms and garlic and cook, stirring constantly, for 5 minutes. Drain well.

4 Stir the mushrooms and garlic into the potatoes, together with the beaten egg and chives.

5 Divide the mixture equally into 4 portions and shape them into round cakes. Toss them in the flour until the outsides of the cakes are completely coated.

6 Heat the oil in a frying pan. Add the potato cakes and fry over a medium heat for 10 minutes until they are golden brown, turning them over halfway through. Serve the cakes at once, with a simple crisp salad.

COOK'S TIP

Prepare the cakes in advance, cover and leave to chill in the refrigerator for up to 24 hours, if you wish.

Cheese & Onion Rostis

These grated potato cakes are also known as straw cakes, because they resemble a straw mat. Serve them with a tomato sauce or salad.

NUTRITIONAL INFORMATION

Calories	307	Sugars	........4g
Protein	.........8g	Fat	..........13g
Carbohydrate	...42g	Saturates	.......6g

10 mins   40 mins

SERVES 4

INGREDIENTS

900 g/2 lb potatoes

1 onion, grated

50 g/1¾ oz Gruyère cheese, grated

2 tbsp chopped parsley

1 tbsp olive oil

2 tbsp butter

salt and pepper

TO GARNISH

1 spring onion, shredded

1 small tomato, quartered

1 Parboil the potatoes in a pan of lightly salted boiling water for 10 minutes and leave to cool. Peel the potatoes and grate with a coarse grater. Place the grated potatoes in a large mixing bowl.

COOK'S TIP

The potato cakes should be flattened as much as possible during cooking, otherwise the outsides will be cooked before the centres are done.

2 Stir in the onion, cheese and parsley. Season well with salt and pepper. Divide the potato mixture into 4 portions of equal size and form them into cakes.

3 Heat half of the olive oil and butter in a frying pan and cook two of the potato cakes over a high heat for 1 minute, then reduce the heat and cook

for 5 minutes, until they are golden underneath. Turn them over and cook for a further 5 minutes.

4 Repeat with the other half of the oil and the remaining butter to cook the remaining 2 cakes. Transfer to warm individual serving plates, garnish and serve immediately.

Potato & Cauliflower Fritters

These fritters make a filling snack. They are a great way to use up leftover cooked vegetables.

NUTRITIONAL INFORMATION

Calories 665	Sugars 5g	
Protein 18g	Fat 25g	
Carbohydrate . . .98g	Saturates 4g	

 10 mins   15–20 mins

SERVES 4

I N G R E D I E N T S

225 g/8 oz floury potatoes, diced

225 g/8 oz cauliflower florets

35 g/1¼ oz Parmesan cheese, freshly grated

1 egg

1 egg white for coating

oil, for frying

paprika, for dusting (optional)

salt and pepper

crispy bacon slices, chopped, to serve

1 Cook the potatoes in a saucepan of boiling water for 10 minutes until cooked through. Drain well and mash.

2 Meanwhile, cook the cauliflower florets in a separate pan of boiling water for 10 minutes.

3 Drain the cauliflower florets and mix into the mashed potato. Stir in the Parmesan cheese and season well with salt and pepper.

4 Separate the whole egg and beat the yolk into the potato and cauliflower, mixing well.

5 Lightly whisk both the egg whites in a clean bowl, then carefully fold into the potato and cauliflower mixture.

6 Divide the potato mixture into eight equal portions and then shape them into rounds.

7 Heat the oil in a frying pan and cook the fritters for 3–5 minutes, turning once halfway through cooking.

8 Dust the cooked fritters with a little paprika, if desired, and then serve them at once accompanied by the crispy chopped bacon.

VARIATION

Any other vegetable, such as broccoli, can be used in this recipe instead of the cauliflower florets, if you prefer.

Fritters with Garlic Sauce

Chunks of cooked potato are coated first in Parmesan cheese, then in a light batter before being fried until golden for a delicious hot snack.

NUTRITIONAL INFORMATION

Calories 599   Sugars 9g
Protein . . . . .22g   Fat 39g
Carbohydrate . . .42g   Saturates 13g

20 mins   20–25 mins

SERVES 4

I N G R E D I E N T S

500 g/1 lb 2 oz waxy potatoes, cubed

125 g/4½ oz Parmesan cheese, freshly grated

vegetable oil, for deep-frying

S A U C E

2 tbsp butter

1 onion, halved and sliced

2 garlic cloves, crushed

2½ tbsp plain flour

300 ml/10 fl oz milk

1 tbsp chopped parsley

B A T T E R

5 tbsp plain flour

1 small egg

150 ml/5 fl oz milk

1 To make the sauce, melt the butter in a saucepan and cook the onion and garlic over a low heat, stirring frequently, for 2–3 minutes. Add the flour and cook, stirring constantly, for 1 minute.

2 Remove from the heat and stir in the milk and parsley. Return to the heat and bring to the boil. Keep warm.

3 Meanwhile, cook the cubed potatoes in a saucepan of boiling water for 5–10 minutes, until just firm. Do not overcook or they will fall apart.

4 Drain the potatoes and toss them in the Parmesan cheese. If the potatoes are still slightly wet, the cheese will stick to them and coat them well.

5 To make the batter, place the flour in a mixing bowl and gradually beat in the egg and milk until smooth. Dip the potato cubes into the batter to coat them.

6 In a large saucepan or deep-fryer, heat the oil to 180°C/350°F or until a cube of bread browns in 30 seconds. Add the fritters and cook for 3–4 minutes, or until golden.

7 Remove the fritters with a slotted spoon and drain well. Transfer them to a warm serving bowl and serve immediately with the garlic sauce.

Hash Browns & Tomato Sauce

Hash Browns are a popular American recipe of fried potato squares, often served as brunch. This recipe includes extra vegetables.

NUTRITIONAL INFORMATION

Calories . . . . .339 Sugars 9g
Protein . . . . .10g Fat 21g
Carbohydrate . . .29g Saturates 7g

 20 mins   45 mins

SERVES 4

I N G R E D I E N T S

500 g/1 lb 2 oz waxy potatoes

1 carrot, diced

1 celery stick, diced

55 g/2 oz button mushrooms, diced

1 onion, diced

2 garlic cloves, crushed

25 g/1 oz frozen peas, thawed

55 g/2 oz Parmesan cheese, freshly grated

4 tbsp vegetable oil

2 tbsp butter

salt and pepper

S A U C E

300 ml/10 fl oz passata

2 tbsp chopped fresh coriander

1 tbsp vegetarian Worcester sauce

½ tsp chilli powder

2 tsp brown sugar

2 tsp American mustard

75 ml/2½ fl oz vegetable stock

1 Cook the potatoes in a saucepan of lightly salted boiling water for 10 minutes. Drain and leave to cool. Meanwhile, cook the carrot in lightly salted boiling water for 5 minutes.

2 When the potatoes are cool enough to handle, grate them with a coarse grater.

3 Drain the carrot and add it to the grated potatoes, together with the celery, mushrooms, onion, garlic, peas and cheese. Season to taste with salt and pepper.

4 Put all of the sauce ingredients in a small saucepan and bring to the boil. Reduce the heat to low and simmer for 15 minutes.

5 Divide the potato mixture into 8 portions of equal size and shape into flattened rectangles with your hands.

6 Heat the oil and butter in a frying pan and cook the hash browns in batches over a low heat for 4–5 minutes on each side, until crisp and golden brown.

7 Transfer the hash browns to a serving plate and serve immediately with the tomato sauce.

Feta & Spinach Omelette

This quick chunky omelette has pieces of potato cooked into the egg mixture and is then filled with feta cheese and spinach.

NUTRITIONAL INFORMATION

Calories 564	Sugars 6g
Protein 30g	Fat 39g
Carbohydrate ...25g	Saturates 19g

 20 mins   25–30 mins

SERVES 4

INGREDIENTS

75 g/2¾ oz butter

1.3 kg/3 lb waxy potatoes, diced

3 garlic cloves, crushed

1 tsp paprika

2 tomatoes, peeled, deseeded and diced

12 eggs

pepper

FILLING

225 g/8 oz baby spinach

1 tsp fennel seeds

125 g/4½ oz feta cheese, diced (drained weight)

4 tbsp natural yogurt

1 Heat 25 g/1 oz of the butter in a frying pan and cook the potatoes over a low heat, stirring constantly, for 7–10 minutes until golden. Transfer to a bowl.

2 Add the garlic, paprika and tomatoes to the pan and cook for a further 2 minutes.

3 Whisk the eggs together and season with pepper. Pour the eggs into the potatoes and mix well.

4 Cook the spinach in boiling water for 1 minute, until just wilted. Drain and refresh under cold running water. Pat dry with kitchen paper. Stir in the fennel seeds, feta cheese and yogurt.

5 Heat a quarter of the remaining butter in a 15-cm/6-inch omelette pan. Ladle a quarter of the egg and potato mixture into the pan. Cook, turning once, for 2 minutes, until set.

6 Transfer the omelette to a serving plate. Spoon a quarter of the spinach mixture on to one half of the omelette, then fold the omelette in half over the filling. Repeat to make 4 omelettes.

VARIATION

Use any other cheese, such as blue cheese, instead of the feta, and blanched broccoli in place of the baby spinach, if you prefer.

Spanish Tortilla

This classic Spanish dish is often served as part of a *tapas* selection.
A variety of cooked vegetables can be added to this recipe.

NUTRITIONAL INFORMATION

Calories 430	Sugars 6g
Protein 16g	Fat 20g
Carbohydrate ...50g	Saturates 4g

10 mins   35 mins

SERVES 4

I N G R E D I E N T S

1 kg/2 lb 4 oz waxy potatoes, thinly sliced

4 tbsp vegetable oil

1 onion, sliced

2 garlic cloves, crushed

1 green pepper, deseeded and diced

2 tomatoes, deseeded and chopped

25 g/1 oz canned sweetcorn, drained

6 large eggs, beaten

2 tbsp chopped parsley

salt and pepper

1 Parboil the potatoes in a saucepan of lightly salted boiling water for 5 minutes. Drain well.

2 Heat the oil in a large frying pan, add the potatoes and onion and

then sauté over a low heat, stirring constantly, for 5 minutes, until the potatoes have browned.

3 Add the garlic, pepper, tomatoes and sweetcorn, mixing well.

4 Pour in the eggs and add the parsley. Season well with salt and pepper. Cook for 10–12 minutes, until the underside is cooked through.

5 Remove the frying pan from the heat and continue to cook the tortilla under a preheated medium grill for 5–7 minutes, or until the tortilla is set and the top is golden brown.

6 Cut the tortilla into wedges or cubes, depending on your preference, and transfer to serving dishes. Serve with salad. In Spain tortillas are served hot, cold or warm.

COOK'S TIP

Ensure that the handle of your pan is heatproof before placing it under the grill and be sure to use an oven glove when removing it because it will be very hot.

Paprika Crisps

These wafer-thin potato crisps are great cooked over a barbecue and served with spicy vegetable kebabs.

NUTRITIONAL INFORMATION

Calories 149   Sugars 0.6g
Protein . . . . .2g   Fat 8g
Carbohydrate . . .17g   Saturates 1g

 5 mins   7 mins

SERVES 4

I N G R E D I E N T S

2 large potatoes

3 tbsp olive oil

½ tsp paprika

salt

1 Using a sharp knife, slice the potatoes very thinly so that they are almost transparent. Drain the potato slices thoroughly and pat dry with kitchen paper.

2 Heat the oil in a large frying pan and add the paprika, stirring constantly to ensure that the paprika doesn't catch and burn.

3 Add the potato slices to the frying pan and cook them in a single layer for about 5 minutes or until the potato slices just begin to curl slightly at the edges.

VARIATION

You could use curry powder or any other spice to flavour the crisps instead of the paprika, if you prefer.

4 Remove the potato slices from the pan using a slotted spoon and transfer them to kitchen paper to drain thoroughly.

5 Thread the potato slices on to several wooden kebab skewers.

6 Sprinkle the potato slices with a little salt and cook over a medium hot barbecue or under a medium grill, turning frequently, for 10 minutes, until the potato slices begin to go crisp. Sprinkle with a little more salt, if preferred, and serve immediately.

Creamy Stuffed Mushrooms

These oven-baked mushrooms are covered with a creamy potato and mushroom filling topped with melted cheese.

NUTRITIONAL INFORMATION

Calories	...214	Sugars	...1g
Protein	...5g	Fat	...17g
Carbohydrate	...11g	Saturates	...11g

20 mins, plus 20 mins soaking time   40 mins

SERVES 4

INGREDIENTS

25 g/1 oz dried ceps

225 g/8 oz floury potatoes, diced

2 tbsp butter, melted

4 tbsp double cream

2 tbsp chopped fresh chives

8 large open-capped mushrooms

25 g/1 oz Emmenthal cheese, grated

150 ml/5 fl oz vegetable stock

salt and pepper

fresh chives, to garnish

1 Place the dried ceps in a small bowl. Add sufficient boiling water to cover and set aside to soak for 20 minutes.

2 Meanwhile, cook the potatoes in a medium saucepan of lightly salted boiling water for 10 minutes, until cooked through and tender. Drain well and mash until smooth.

3 Drain the soaked ceps and then chop them finely. Mix them into the mashed potato.

4 Thoroughly blend the butter, cream and chives together and pour the mixture into the ceps and potato mixture, mixing well. Season to taste with salt and pepper.

5 Remove the stalks from the open-capped mushrooms. Chop the stalks and stir them into the potato mixture. Spoon the mixture into the open-capped mushrooms and sprinkle the cheese over the top.

6 Arrange the filled mushrooms in a shallow ovenproof dish and pour in the vegetable stock.

7 Cover the dish and cook in a preheated oven, 220°C/425°F/Gas Mark 7, for 20 minutes. Remove the lid and cook for 5 minutes until golden.

8 Garnish the mushrooms with fresh chives and serve at once.

VARIATION

Use fresh mushrooms instead of the dried ceps, if preferred, and stir a mixture of chopped nuts into the mushroom stuffing mixture for extra crunch.

Potato & Mushroom Bake

Use any mixture of mushrooms for this creamy layered bake.
It can be served straight from the dish in which it is cooked.

NUTRITIONAL INFORMATION

Calories 304	Sugars 2g	
Protein 4g	Fat 24g	
Carbohydrate . . .20g	Saturates 15g	

 15 mins   1 hr

SERVES 4

INGREDIENTS

2 tbsp butter

500 g/1 lb 2 oz waxy potatoes, thinly sliced

150 g/5½ oz sliced mixed mushrooms

1 tbsp chopped rosemary

4 tbsp chopped chives

2 garlic cloves, crushed

150 ml/5 fl oz double cream

salt and pepper

snipped chives, to garnish

1 Grease a shallow round ovenproof dish with the butter.

2 Parboil the potatoes in a saucepan of boiling water for 10 minutes. Drain well. Layer a quarter of the potatoes in the base of the dish.

3 Arrange one-quarter of the mushrooms on top of the potatoes and sprinkle with one-quarter of the rosemary, chives and garlic. Continue making layers in the same order, finishing with a layer of potatoes on top.

4 Pour the cream over the top of the potatoes. Season to taste with salt and pepper.

5 Cook in a preheated oven, 190°C/375°F/Gas Mark 5, for about 45 minutes, or until the bake is golden brown and piping hot.

6 Garnish with snipped chives and serve at once straight from the dish.

COOK'S TIP

For a special occasion, the bake may be made in a lined cake tin and then turned out to serve.

Spicy Chickpea Snack

You can use fresh chickpeas, soaked overnight, for this popular Indian snack, but the canned variety is just as flavoursome.

NUTRITIONAL INFORMATION

Calories 190	Sugars 4g
Protein 9g	Fat 3g
Carbohydrate ...34g	Saturates 0.3g

 5 mins   10 mins

SERVES 4

INGREDIENTS

400 g/14 oz canned chickpeas, drained

450 g/1 lb potatoes

1 medium onion

2 tbsp tamarind paste

6 tbsp water

1 tsp chilli powder

2 tsp sugar

1 tsp salt

TO GARNISH

1 tomato, sliced

2 fresh green chillies, chopped

fresh coriander leaves

1 Place the chickpeas in a bowl. Using a sharp knife, cut the potatoes into small cubes.

COOK'S TIP

Chickpeas have a nutty flavour and slightly crunchy texture. Indian cooks also grind these to make a flour called gram or besan, which is used to make breads, thicken sauces, and to make batters for deep-fried dishes.

2 Place the potatoes in a saucepan of water and boil until cooked through. Test by inserting the tip of a knife into the potatoes – they should feel soft and tender. Set the potatoes aside.

3 Using a sharp knife, finely chop the onion. Set aside until required.

4 Mix together the tamarind paste and water. Add the chilli powder, sugar and salt and mix again. Pour the mixture over the chickpeas.

5 Add the onion and the diced potatoes, and stir to mix. Season to taste.

6 Transfer to a serving bowl and garnish with the tomato, chillies and coriander leaves.

Crispy Potato Skins

Use the potato flesh in this recipe for another meal, so make slightly more than you need. They make a delicious starter and are ideal for a barbecue.

NUTRITIONAL INFORMATION

Calories 395	Sugars 2g
Protein 12g	Fat 20g
Carbohydrate ...44g	Saturates 9g

 2 mins   1 hr 15 mins

SERVES 4

INGREDIENTS

8 small baking potatoes, scrubbed

4 tbsp butter, melted

salt and pepper

OPTIONAL TOPPING

6 spring onions, sliced

50 g/1¾ oz Gruyère cheese, grated

50 g/1¾ oz salami, cut into thin strips

1 Preheat the oven to 200°C/400°F/Gas Mark 6. Prick the potatoes with a fork and bake for 1 hour or until tender.

2 Cut the potatoes in half and scoop out the flesh, leaving about 5 mm/ ¼ inch potato flesh lining the skin.

3 Brush the insides of the potato with melted butter.

4 Place the skins, cut-side down, over medium hot coals and barbecue (or grill) for 10–15 minutes.

5 Turn the potato skins over and barbecue (or grill) for a further 5 minutes or until they are crispy. Take care that they do not burn.

6 Season the potato skins with salt and pepper to taste and serve while they are still warm.

7 If wished, the skins can be filled with a variety of toppings. Barbecue (or grill) the potato skins as above for about 10 minutes, then turn cut-side up and sprinkle with slices of spring onion, grated cheese and chopped salami. Barbecue (or grill) for a further 5 minutes until the cheese begins to melt. Serve hot.

COOK'S TIP
Potato skins can be served on their own but they are delicious served with a dip. Try a spicy tomato or hummus dip.

Potatoes with Goat's Cheese

This makes a luscious side dish to serve with meat, or a satisfying vegetarian main course. Goat's cheese is a traditional food of Mexico.

NUTRITIONAL INFORMATION

Calories 725   Sugars 4g
Protein ....30g   Fat 43g
Carbohydrate ...56g   Saturates 28g

 2 mins   35 mins

SERVES 4

INGREDIENTS

1.25 kg/2 lb 12 oz baking potatoes, peeled and cut into chunks

pinch of salt

pinch of sugar

200 ml/7 fl oz crème fraîche

125 ml/4 fl oz vegetable or chicken stock

3 garlic cloves, finely chopped

a few shakes of bottled chipotle salsa, or 1 dried chipotle, reconstituted, deseeded and thinly sliced

225 g/8 oz goat's cheese, sliced

175 g/6 oz mozzarella or Cheddar cheese, grated

50 g/1¾ oz Parmesan or pecorino cheese, grated

salt

1 Put the potatoes in a pan of water with the salt and sugar. Bring to the boil and cook for about 10 minutes until they are half cooked.

2 Combine the crème fraîche with the stock, garlic and chipotle salsa.

3 Arrange half the potatoes in a casserole. Pour half the crème fraîche sauce over the potatoes and cover with

the goat's cheese. Top with the remaining potatoes and the sauce.

4 Sprinkle with the grated mozzarella or Cheddar cheese, then with either the grated Parmesan or pecorino.

5 Bake in a preheated oven at 180°C/350°F/Gas Mark 4 for approximately 25 minutes, until the potatoes are tender and the cheese topping is lightly golden and has become crisp in places. Serve immediately.

Smoked Fish & Potato Pâté

This smoked fish pâté is given a tart fruity flavour by the gooseberries, which complement the fish perfectly.

NUTRITIONAL INFORMATION

Calories	418	Sugars	.....4g
Protein	.....18g	Fat	.....25g
Carbohydrate	...32g	Saturates	.....6g

 20 mins   10 mins

SERVES 4

I N G R E D I E N T S

650 g/1 lb 7 oz floury potatoes, diced

300 g/10½ oz smoked mackerel, skinned and flaked

75 g/2¾ oz cooked gooseberries

2 tsp lemon juice

2 tbsp low-fat crème fraîche

1 tbsp capers

1 gherkin, chopped

1 tbsp chopped dill pickle

1 tbsp chopped fresh dill

salt and pepper

lemon wedges, to garnish

toast or warm crusty bread, to serve

1 Cook the diced potatoes in a saucepan of boiling water for 10 minutes until tender, then drain well.

2 Place the cooked potatoes in a food processor or blender.

3 Add the skinned and flaked smoked mackerel and process for 30 seconds until fairly smooth. Alternatively, place the ingredients in a bowl and then mash them with a fork.

4 Add the cooked gooseberries, lemon juice and crème fraîche to the fish

and potato mixture. Blend for a further 10 seconds or mash well.

5 Stir in the capers, gherkin, dill pickle, and fresh dill. Season well with salt and pepper.

6 Turn the fish pâté into a serving dish, garnish with lemon wedges and serve with slices of toast or warm crusty bread cut into chunks or slices.

COOK'S TIP
Use stewed, canned or bottled cooked gooseberries for convenience and to save time, or when fresh gooseberries are out of season.

Potato Kibbeh

Kibbeh is a Middle Eastern dish, traditionally made with cracked wheat, lamb and spices. Serve with tahini, salad and warm Middle Eastern bread.

NUTRITIONAL INFORMATION

Calories	600	Sugars	........4g
Protein	........20g	Fat	..........35g
Carbohydrate	...53g	Saturates	.......8g

10 mins, plus 30 mins soaking time   20 mins

SERVES 4

INGREDIENTS

175 g/6 oz bulgar wheat

350 g/12 oz floury potatoes, diced

2 small eggs

2 tbsp butter, melted

pinch of ground cumin

pinch of ground coriander

pinch of grated nutmeg

salt and pepper

oil for deep-frying

STUFFING

175 g/6 oz minced lamb

1 small onion, chopped

1 tbsp pine nuts

25 g/1 oz dried apricots, chopped

pinch of grated nutmeg

pinch of ground cinnamon

1 tbsp chopped fresh coriander

2 tbsp lamb stock

1 Put the bulgar wheat in a bowl and cover with boiling water. Soak for 30 minutes until the water has been absorbed and the bulgar wheat has swollen.

2 Meanwhile, cook the diced potatoes in a saucepan of boiling water for 10 minutes or until cooked through. Drain and mash until smooth.

3 Add the bulgar wheat to the mashed potatoes with the eggs, melted butter, cumin, coriander, and nutmeg. Mix well and season with salt and pepper.

4 To make the stuffing, dry fry the lamb for 5 minutes, add the onion and cook for a further 2–3 minutes. Add the remaining stuffing ingredients and cook for 5 minutes until the lamb stock has been absorbed. Leave the mixture to cool slightly, then divide into 8 portions. Roll each one into a ball.

5 Divide the potato mixture into 8 portions and flatten each into a round. Place a portion of stuffing in the centre of each round. Shape the coating around the stuffing to encase it completely.

6 In a large saucepan or deep fat fryer, heat the oil to180°C–190°C/350°F–375°F or until a cube of bread browns in 30 seconds, and cook the kibbeh for 5–7 minutes until golden brown. Drain well and serve at once.

Fish Balls with Tomato Sauce

These spicy potato and fish balls are deep-fried and served with a rich tomato sauce. They can be made in advance and fried just before eating.

NUTRITIONAL INFORMATION

Calories 438   Sugars 4g
Protein ....18g   Fat 32g
Carbohydrate ...23g   Saturates 8g

🧈 5 mins   🕐 40 mins

SERVES 4

I N G R E D I E N T S

450 g/1 lb floury potatoes, diced

3 tbsp butter

225 g/8 oz smoked fish, such as cod, skinned

2 eggs, beaten

1 tbsp chopped fresh dill

½ tsp cayenne pepper

oil for deep-frying

salt and pepper

dill sprigs, to garnish

S A U C E

300 ml/10 fl oz passata

1 tbsp tomato purée

2 tbsp chopped fresh dill

150 ml/5 fl oz fish stock

VARIATION

Smoked fish is used for extra flavour, but white fish fillets or minced prawns may be used, if preferred.

1 Cook the diced potatoes in a saucepan of boiling water for 10 minutes or until cooked. Drain well, then add the butter to the potato and mash until smooth. Season well with salt and pepper.

2 Meanwhile, poach the fish in boiling water for 10 minutes, turning once. Drain and mash the fish. Stir it into the potato mixture and leave to cool.

3 While the potato and fish mixture is cooling, make the sauce. Put the passata, tomato purée, dill and stock in a pan and bring to the boil. Reduce the heat, cover the pan and simmer for 20 minutes until thickened.

4 Add the eggs, dill and cayenne pepper to the potato and fish mixture and beat until well mixed.

5 In a large saucepan or deep fat fryer, heat the oil to 180°C–190°C/350°F–375°F, or until a cube of bread browns in 30 seconds. Drop dessertspoons of the potato mixture into the oil and cook for 3–4 minutes until golden brown. Drain on kitchen paper.

6 Garnish the potato and fish balls with dill and serve with the tomato sauce.

Salmon Pancakes

These pancakes are based on the latke, which is a thin, crisp pancake, and are served with smoked salmon and soured cream for a taste of luxury.

NUTRITIONAL INFORMATION

Calories 142	Sugars 1g
Protein 6.8g	Fat 7.8g
Carbohydrate ..11.9g	Saturates 2.8g

  5 mins   25 mins

SERVES 4

INGREDIENTS

450 g/1 lb floury potatoes, grated

2 spring onions, chopped

2 tbsp self-raising flour

2 eggs, beaten

2 tbsp vegetable oil

salt and pepper

fresh chives, to garnish

TOPPING

150 ml/5 fl oz soured cream

125 g/4½ oz smoked salmon

VARIATION

These pancakes are equally delicious topped with prosciutto or any other dry-cured ham instead of the smoked salmon.

1 Rinse the grated potatoes under cold running water, drain and pat dry on kitchen paper. Transfer to a mixing bowl.

2 Mix the spring onions, flour and eggs into the potatoes and season well with salt and pepper.

3 Heat 1 tablespoon of the oil in a frying pan. Drop about 4 tablespoonfuls of the mixture into the pan and spread each one with the back of a spoon to form a round (the mixture should make 16 pancakes). Cook for 5–7 minutes, turning once, until golden. Drain well.

4 Heat the remaining oil and cook the remaining mixture in batches.

5 Top the pancakes with the soured cream and smoked salmon, garnish with fresh chives and serve hot.

Tuna Fishcakes

These fishcakes make a satisfying and quick mid-week supper. The tomato sauce is flavoured with a tempting combination of lemon, garlic and basil.

NUTRITIONAL INFORMATION

Calories	638	Sugars	.........5g
Protein	........35g	Fat	..........40g
Carbohydrate	...38g	Saturates	.......5g

 5 mins   1 hr 10 mins

SERVES 4

I N G R E D I E N T S

225 g/8 oz potatoes, cubed

1 tbsp olive oil

1 large shallot, finely chopped

1 garlic clove, finely chopped

1 tsp thyme leaves

400 g//14 oz canned tuna in olive oil, drained

grated rind ½ lemon

1 tbsp chopped fresh parsley

2–3 tbsp plain flour

1 egg, lightly beaten

115 g/4 oz fresh breadcrumbs

vegetable oil, for shallow frying

salt and pepper

Q U I C K   T O M A T O   S A U C E

2 tbsp olive oil

400 g/14 oz canned chopped tomatoes

1 garlic clove, crushed

½ tsp sugar

grated rind ½ lemon

1 tbsp chopped fresh basil

salt and pepper

1 For the tuna fishcakes, cook the potatoes in plenty of boiling salted water for 12–15 minutes until tender. Mash, leaving a few lumps, and set aside.

2 Heat the oil in a small frying pan and cook the shallot gently for 5 minutes until softened. Add the garlic and thyme leaves and cook for an additional minute. Allow to cool slightly then add to the potatoes with the tuna, lemon rind, parsley and seasoning. Mix together well but leave some texture.

3 Form the mixture into 6–8 cakes. Dip the cakes first in the flour, then the egg and finally the breadcrumbs to coat. Refrigerate for 30 minutes.

4 For the tomato sauce, put the olive oil, tomatoes, garlic, sugar, lemon rind, basil and seasoning into a saucepan and bring to the boil. Cover and simmer for 30 minutes. Uncover and simmer for 15 minutes until thickened.

5 Heat enough oil in a frying pan to cover the bottom generously. Fry the fishcakes in batches for 3–4 minutes each side until golden and crisp. Drain on kitchen paper while you fry the remaining fishcakes. Serve hot with the tomato sauce.

Thai Potato Crab Cakes

These small crab cakes are based on a traditional Thai recipe. They make a delicious snack when served with this sweet and sour cucumber sauce.

NUTRITIONAL INFORMATION

Calories	254	Sugars	.........9g
Protein	........12g	Fat	...........6g
Carbohydrate	...40g	Saturates	......1g

10 mins   30 mins

SERVES 4

I N G R E D I E N T S

450 g/1 lb floury potatoes, diced

175 g/6 oz white crab meat, drained if canned

4 spring onions, chopped

1 tsp light soy sauce

½ tsp sesame oil

1 tsp chopped lemon grass

1 tsp lime juice

3 tbsp plain flour

2 tbsp vegetable oil

salt and pepper

S A U C E

4 tbsp finely chopped cucumber

2 tbsp clear honey

1 tbsp garlic wine vinegar

½ tsp light soy sauce

1 chopped red chilli

TO GARNISH

1 red chilli, sliced

cucumber slices

1 Cook the diced potatoes in a saucepan of boiling water for 10 minutes until cooked through. Drain well and mash.

2 Mix the crab meat into the potatoes with the spring onions, soy sauce, sesame oil, lemon grass, lime juice and flour. Season with salt and pepper.

3 Divide the potato mixture into 8 portions of equal size and shape them into small rounds, using floured hands.

4 Heat the oil in a wok or frying pan and cook the cakes, four at a time, for 5–7 minutes, turning once. Keep warm and repeat with the remaining crab cakes.

5 Meanwhile, make the sauce. In a small serving bowl, mix the cucumber, honey, vinegar, soy sauce and red chilli.

6 Garnish the cakes with the sliced red chilli and cucumber slices and serve with the sauce.

Prawn Rostis

These crisp little vegetable and prawn cakes make an ideal light lunch or supper, accompanied by a salad.

NUTRITIONAL INFORMATION

Calories 445	Sugars 9g
Protein 19g	Fat 29g
Carbohydrate ...29g	Saturates 4g

10 mins   1 hr

SERVES 4

INGREDIENTS

350 g/12 oz potatoes

350 g/12 oz celeriac

1 carrot

½ small onion

225 g/8 oz cooked peeled prawns, thawed if frozen and well-drained on kitchen paper

2½ tbsp plain flour

1 egg, lightly beaten

vegetable oil, for frying

salt and pepper

CHERRY TOMATO SALSA

225 g/8 oz mixed cherry tomatoes such as baby plum, yellow, orange, pear, quartered

½ small mango, finely diced

1 red chilli, deseeded and finely chopped

½ small red onion, finely chopped

1 tbsp chopped fresh coriander

1 tbsp chopped fresh chives

2 tbsp olive oil

2 tsp lemon juice

salt and pepper

1 For the salsa, mix the tomatoes, mango, chilli, onion, coriander, chives, olive oil, lemon juice, and seasoning. Set aside for the flavours to infuse.

2 Using a food processor or the fine blade of a box grater, finely grate the potatoes, celeriac, carrot and onion. Mix together with the prawns, flour and egg. Season well and set aside.

3 Divide the prawn mixture into eight equal pieces. Press each into a greased 10-cm/4-inch cutter (if you only have one cutter, you can simply shape the rostis individually).

4 In a large frying pan, heat a shallow layer of oil. When hot, transfer the vegetable cakes, still in the cutters, to the frying pan, in four batches if necessary. When the oil sizzles underneath, remove the cutter. Fry gently, pressing down with a spatula, for 6–8 minutes on each side, until crisp and browned and the vegetables are tender. Drain on kitchen paper and keep warm in a preheated oven. Serve hot with the tomato salsa.

Spicy Fish & Potato Fritters

You need nice, floury-textured old potatoes for making these tasty fritters. Any white fish of your choice may be used.

NUTRITIONAL INFORMATION

Calories ....349 Sugars 4g
Protein ....31g Fat 8g
Carbohydrate ...41g Saturates 1g

15 mins   25 mins

SERVES 4

INGREDIENTS

500 g/1 lb 2 oz potatoes, peeled and cut into even-sized pieces

500g/1 lb 2 oz white fish fillets, such as cod or haddock, skinned and boned

6 spring onions, sliced

1 fresh green chilli, deseeded

2 garlic cloves, peeled

1 tsp salt

1 tbsp medium or hot curry paste

2 eggs, beaten

150 g/5½ oz fresh white breadcrumbs

vegetable oil, for shallow frying

mango chutney, to serve

TO GARNISH

coriander sprigs and lime wedges

1 Cook the potatoes in a pan of boiling, salted water until tender. Drain well, return the potatoes to the pan and place over a moderate heat for a few moments to dry off. Cool slightly, then place in a food processor with the fish, onions, chilli, garlic, salt and curry paste. Process until the ingredients are very finely chopped and blended.

2 Turn out the potato mixture into a bowl and mix in 2 tablespoons of beaten egg and 55 g/2 oz of the breadcrumbs. Place the remaining beaten egg and breadcrumbs in separate dishes.

3 Divide the potato mixture into eight equal portions and, using a spoon to help you (the mixture is quite soft), dip each potato portion first in the beaten egg and then coat it in the breadcrumbs. When each portion is evenly coated, carefully shape it into an oval.

4 Heat enough oil in a large frying pan for shallow frying. When the oil has reached the required temperature, fry the fritters over moderate heat for 3–4 minutes, turning frequently, until golden brown and cooked through.

5 Drain on absorbent kitchen paper and garnish with lime wedges and coriander sprigs. Serve the fritters hot, with mango chutney.

Chicken & Almond Rissoles

Cooked potatoes and cooked chicken are combined to make tasty rissoles rolled in chopped almonds then served with stir-fried vegetables.

NUTRITIONAL INFORMATION

Calories 161   Sugars 3g

Protein . . . . .12g   Fat 9g

Carbohydrate . . . .8g   Saturates 1g

35 mins   20 mins

SERVES 4

INGREDIENTS

125 g/4½ oz parboiled potatoes

1 carrot

125 g/4½ oz cooked chicken

1 garlic clove, crushed

½ tsp dried tarragon or thyme

generous pinch of ground allspice or ground coriander seeds

1 egg yolk, or ½ egg, beaten

about 25 g/1 oz flaked almonds

salt and pepper

STIR-FRIED VEGETABLES

1 celery stick

2 spring onions, trimmed

1 tbsp oil

8 baby sweetcorn cobs

40 g/1½ oz mangetouts or sugar snap peas, topped and tailed

2 tsp balsamic vinegar

salt and pepper

2 Add the egg and bind the ingredients together. Divide in half and shape into sausages. Chop the almonds and then evenly coat each rissole in the nuts. Place the rissoles in a greased ovenproof dish and cook in a preheated oven, 200°C/400°F/Gas Mark 6, for about 20 minutes until browned.

3 To prepare the stir-fried vegetables, cut the celery and spring onions on the diagonal into narrow slices. Heat the oil in a frying pan and toss in the vegetables. Cook over a high heat for 1–2 minutes, then add the sweetcorn cobs and mangetouts or sugar snap peas, and cook for 2–3 minutes. Finally, add the balsamic vinegar and season to taste with salt and pepper.

4 Place the rissoles on serving plates and add the stir-fried vegetables.

1 Grate the parboiled potatoes and raw carrots coarsely into a bowl. Chop finely or mince the chicken. Add to the vegetables with the garlic, herbs and spices and plenty of salt and pepper.

Chicken & Herb Fritters

These fritters are delicious served with salad greens, a fresh vegetable salsa or a chilli sauce dip.

NUTRITIONAL INFORMATION

Calories ....333 Sugars 1g
Protein ....16g Fat 23g
Carbohydrate ...17g Saturates 5g

  5 mins 10–15 mins

SERVES 4

INGREDIENTS

500 g/1 lb 2 oz mashed potato, with butter added

225 g/8 oz chopped, cooked chicken

115 g/4 oz cooked ham, finely chopped

1 tbsp mixed herbs

2 eggs, lightly beaten

milk

fresh brown breadcrumbs

oil, for shallow frying

salt and pepper

sprig of fresh parsley, to garnish

salad greens, to serve

COOK'S TIP
A mixture of chopped fresh tarragon and parsley makes a fresh and flavoursome addition to these tasty fritters.

1 In a large bowl, blend the potatoes, chicken, ham, herbs and 1 egg, and season well.

2 Shape the mixture into small balls or flat pancakes.

3 Add a little milk to the second egg and mix together.

4 Place the breadcrumbs on a plate. Dip the balls in the egg and milk mixture, then roll in the breadcrumbs to coat them completely.

5 Heat the cooking oil in a large frying pan and fry the fritters until they are golden brown. Garnish with a sprig of fresh parsley and serve at once with fresh salad greens.

Chicken & Cheese Jackets

Use the breasts from a roasted chicken to make these delicious potatoes and serve as a light lunch or supper dish.

NUTRITIONAL INFORMATION

Calories 417   Sugars 4g
Protein . . . . .28g   Fat 10g
Carbohydrate . . .57g   Saturates 5g

 10 mins   ⏱ 50 mins

SERVES 4

I N G R E D I E N T S

4 large baking potatoes

225 g/8 oz cooked, boneless chicken breasts

4 spring onions

250 g/9 oz low-fat soft cheese or Quark

pepper

1 Scrub the potatoes and pat dry with absorbent kitchen paper.

2 Prick the potatoes all over with a fork. Bake in a preheated oven, 200°C/400°F/Gas Mark 6, for about 50 minutes until tender.

3 Using a sharp knife, dice the chicken and trim and thickly slice the spring onions. Place the chicken and spring onions in a bowl.

4 Add the low-fat soft cheese or Quark to the chicken and spring onions and stir well to combine.

5 Cut a cross through the top of each potato and pull slightly apart. Spoon the chicken filling into the potatoes and sprinkle with pepper.

6 Serve the chicken and cheese jackets immediately with coleslaw, green salad or a mixed salad.

COOK'S TIP

Look for Quark in the chilled section of the supermarket. It is a low-fat, white, fresh curd cheese made from cow's milk with a delicate, slightly sour flavour.

Meatballs in Spicy Sauce

These meatballs are delicious served with warm crusty bread to 'mop up' the spicy sauce.

NUTRITIONAL INFORMATION

Calories 95   Sugars 2.7g
Protein . . . . .4.5g   Fat 5.8g
Carbohydrate . . .6.6g   Saturates 2.3g

5 mins   1 hr 10 mins

SERVES 4

I N G R E D I E N T S

225 g/8 oz floury potatoes, diced

225 g/8 oz minced beef or lamb

1 onion, finely chopped

1 tbsp chopped fresh coriander

1 celery stick, finely chopped

2 garlic cloves, crushed

2 tbsp butter

1 tbsp vegetable oil

salt and pepper

chopped fresh coriander, to garnish

S A U C E

1 tbsp vegetable oil

1 onion, finely chopped

2 tsp soft brown sugar

400 g/14 oz canned chopped tomatoes

1 green chilli, chopped

1 tsp paprika

150 ml/5 fl oz vegetable stock

2 tsp cornflour

1 Cook the diced potatoes in a saucepan of boiling water for 25 minutes until cooked through. Drain well and transfer to a large mixing bowl. Mash until smooth.

2 Add the minced beef or lamb, onion, coriander, celery and garlic and mix together well.

3 Bring the mixture together with your hands and roll it into 20 small balls.

4 To make the sauce, heat the oil in a pan and sauté the onion for 5 minutes. Add the remaining sauce ingredients and bring to the boil, stirring constantly. Lower the heat and simmer for 20 minutes.

5 Meanwhile, heat the butter and oil for the meatballs in a frying pan. Add the balls in batches and cook for 10–15 minutes until browned, turning frequently. Keep warm whilst cooking the remainder. Serve the meatballs in a warm, shallow ovenproof dish with the sauce poured around them and garnished with the fresh coriander.

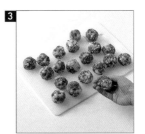

COOK'S TIP

Make the meatballs in advance and chill or freeze them for later use. Make sure you defrost them thoroughly before cooking.

Croquettes with Ham

This classic potato dish may be served plain as an accompaniment or with added ingredients and a cheese sauce as a snack.

NUTRITIONAL INFORMATION

Calories	792	Sugars	.........8g
Protein	........28g	Fat	..........54g
Carbohydrate	...53g	Saturates	......21g

5 mins   30 mins

SERVES 4

I N G R E D I E N T S

450 g/1 lb floury potatoes, diced

300 ml/10 fl oz milk

2 tbsp butter

4 spring onions, chopped

75 g/2¾ oz Cheddar cheese, grated

50 g/1¾ oz smoked ham, chopped

1 celery stick, diced

1 egg, beaten

5 tbsp plain flour

oil, for deep frying

salt and pepper

C O A T I N G

2 eggs, beaten

125 g/4½ oz fresh wholemeal breadcrumbs

S A U C E

2 tbsp butter

2 tbsp plain flour

150 ml/5 fl oz milk

150 ml/5 fl oz vegetable stock

75 g/2¾ oz Cheddar cheese, grated

1 tsp Dijon mustard

1 tbsp chopped fresh coriander

1 Place the potatoes in a pan with the milk and bring to the boil. Reduce to a simmer until the liquid has been absorbed and the potatoes are cooked.

2 Add the butter and mash the potatoes. Stir in the spring onions, cheese, ham, celery, egg and flour. Season and leave to cool.

3 To make the coating, whisk the eggs in a bowl. Put the breadcrumbs in a separate bowl.

4 Shape the potato mixture into 8 balls. First dip them in the egg, then in the breadcrumbs.

5 To make the sauce, melt the butter in a small pan. Add the flour and cook for 1 minute. Remove from the heat and stir in the milk, stock, cheese, mustard and coriander. Bring to the boil, stirring until thickened. Reduce the heat and keep warm, stirring occasionally.

6 In a deep fat fryer, heat the oil to 180°C–190°C/350°F–375°F and fry the croquettes in batches for 5 minutes until golden. Drain well and serve with the sauce.

Noodles with Cheese Sauce

Potatoes are used to make a 'pasta' dough, which is cut into thin noodles, boiled and served with a creamy bacon and mushroom sauce.

NUTRITIONAL INFORMATION

Calories 213   Sugars 1.6g
Protein . . . . .5.3g   Fat 13.5g
Carbohydrate . .18.7g   Saturates 7.4g

5 mins   20 mins

SERVES 4

I N G R E D I E N T S

450 g/1 lb floury potatoes, diced

225 g/8 oz plain flour

1 egg, beaten

1 tbsp milk

salt and pepper

parsley sprig, to garnish

S A U C E

1 tbsp vegetable oil

1 onion, chopped

1 garlic clove, crushed

125 g/4½ oz open-capped mushrooms, sliced

3 smoked bacon slices, chopped

50 g/1¾ oz Parmesan cheese, freshly grated

300 ml/10 fl oz double cream

2 tbsp chopped fresh parsley

1 Cook the diced potatoes in a saucepan of boiling water for 10 minutes until cooked through. Drain well. Mash the potatoes until smooth, then beat in the flour, egg and milk. Season with salt and pepper and then bring together to form a stiff paste.

2 On a lightly floured surface, roll out the paste to form a thin sausage shape. Cut the sausage into 2.5-cm/1-inch lengths. Bring a large pan of salted water to the boil, drop in the dough pieces and cook for 3–4 minutes. They will rise to the top when cooked.

3 To make the sauce, heat the oil in a pan and sauté the onion and garlic for 2 minutes. Add the mushrooms and bacon and cook for 5 minutes. Stir in the cheese, cream and parsley, and season.

4 Drain the noodles and transfer to a warm pasta bowl. Spoon the sauce over the top and toss to mix. Garnish with a parsley sprig and serve.

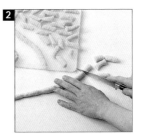

COOK'S TIP

Make the dough in advance, then wrap and store the noodles in the refrigerator for up to 24 hours.

Colcannon

This is an old Irish recipe, usually served with a piece of bacon, but it is equally delicious with a vegetarian main course dish.

NUTRITIONAL INFORMATION

Calories 102   Sugars 4g
Protein . . . . .4g   Fat 4g
Carbohydrate . . .14g   Saturates 2g

  20 mins   20 mins

SERVES 4

I N G R E D I E N T S

225 g/8 oz green cabbage, shredded

5 tbsp milk

225 g/8 oz floury potatoes, diced

1 large leek, chopped

pinch of grated nutmeg

1 tbsp butter, melted

salt and pepper

1 Cook the shredded cabbage in a saucepan of boiling salted water for 7–10 minutes. Drain thoroughly and set aside.

2 Meanwhile, in a separate saucepan, bring the milk to the boil and add the potatoes and leek. Reduce the heat and simmer for 15–20 minutes, or until they are cooked through.

3 Stir in the grated nutmeg and thoroughly mash the potatoes and leek together.

4 Add the drained cabbage to the mashed potato and leek mixture and mix together well.

5 Spoon the mixture into a warmed serving dish, making a hollow in the centre with the back of a spoon.

6 Pour the melted butter into the hollow and serve the colcannon immediately.

COOK'S TIP

There are many different varieties of cabbage, which produce hearts at varying times of year, so you can be sure of being able to make this delicious cabbage dish all year round.

Candied Sweet Potatoes

A taste of the Caribbean is introduced in this recipe, where sweet potatoes are cooked with sugar and lime with a dash of brandy.

NUTRITIONAL INFORMATION

Calories ....348 Sugars 21g
Protein ....3g Fat 9g
Carbohydrate ...67g Saturates 6g

15 mins   25 mins

SERVES 4

INGREDIENTS

675 g/1½ lb sweet potatoes, sliced

3 tbsp butter

1 tbsp lime juice

75 g/2¾ oz soft dark brown sugar

1 tbsp brandy

grated rind of 1 lime

lime wedges, to garnish

1 Cook the sweet potatoes in a saucepan of boiling water for about 5 minutes. Test the potatoes have softened by pricking with a fork. Remove the sweet potatoes with a perforated spoon and drain thoroughly.

2 Melt the butter in a large frying pan. Add the lime juice and brown sugar and heat gently, stirring, to dissolve the sugar.

3 Stir the sweet potatoes and the brandy into the sugar and lime juice mixture. Cook over a low heat for about 10 minutes or until the potato slices are cooked through.

4 Sprinkle the lime rind over the top of the sweet potatoes and mix well.

5 Transfer the candied sweet potatoes to a serving plate. Garnish with lime wedges and serve at once.

COOK'S TIP
Sweet potatoes have a pinkish skin and either white, yellow or orange flesh. It doesn't matter which type is used for this dish.

Fried Potatoes with Onions

Classic fried potatoes are given extra flavour by pre-cooking the potatoes and shallow-frying them in butter with onion, garlic and herbs.

NUTRITIONAL INFORMATION

Calories	140	Sugars	.......1.2g
Protein	........1.8g	Fat	..........8.8g
Carbohydrate	..14.1g	Saturates	.....5.7g

 5 mins   40 mins

SERVES 4

INGREDIENTS

900 g/2 lb waxy potatoes, cubed

125 g/4½ oz butter

1 red onion, cut into 8 pieces

2 garlic cloves, crushed

1 tsp lemon juice

2 tbsp chopped fresh thyme

salt and pepper

1 Cook the cubed potatoes in a saucepan of boiling water for 10 minutes. Drain thoroughly.

2 Melt the butter in a large, heavy-based frying pan and add the red onion wedges, garlic and lemon juice. Cook for 2–3 minutes, stirring.

3 Add the potatoes to the pan and mix well to coat in the butter mixture.

4 Reduce the heat, cover the frying pan and cook for 25–30 minutes or until the potatoes are golden and tender.

5 Sprinkle the chopped thyme over the top of the potatoes and season with salt and pepper to taste.

6 Serve immediately as a side dish to accompany grilled meats or fish.

COOK'S TIP
Onions are used in a multitude of dishes for their pungent flavour. The beautifully coloured purple-red onions used here have a mild, slightly sweet flavour as well as looking extremely attractive. Because of their mild taste, they are equally good eaten raw in salads.

Caramelized New Potatoes

This simple recipe is best served with a plainly cooked main course, because it is fairly sweet and has delicious juices.

NUTRITIONAL INFORMATION

Calories	289	Sugars	........18g
Protein	.........3g	Fat	..........13g
Carbohydrate	...43g	Saturates	.......8g

  5 mins 20 mins

SERVES 4

INGREDIENTS

675 g/1½ lb new potatoes, scrubbed

4 tbsp dark brown sugar

60 g/2 oz butter

1 tbsp orange juice

1 tbsp chopped fresh parsley or coriander

salt and pepper

orange rind curls, to garnish

1 Cook the new potatoes in a saucepan of boiling water for 10 minutes, or until almost tender. Drain thoroughly.

2 Melt all the sugar in a large, heavy-based frying pan over a low heat, stirring constantly.

3 Add the butter and orange juice to the pan, stirring the mixture constantly as the butter melts.

4 Add the potatoes to the orange and butter mixture and continue to cook, turning the potatoes frequently until they are completely coated in the caramel.

5 Sprinkle the chopped fresh parsley or coriander over the potatoes and season according to taste with salt and pepper.

6 Transfer the caramelized new potatoes to a serving dish and garnish with the orange rind. Serve immediately.

VARIATION

Lemon or lime juices may be used instead of the orange juice, if preferred. In addition, garnish the finished dish with pared lemon or lime rind, if desired.

Spanish Potatoes

This type of dish is usually served as a part of Spanish *tapas* and is delicious with salad or a simply-cooked main course dish.

NUTRITIONAL INFORMATION

Calories ....176 Sugars 9g
Protein ....5g Fat 6g
Carbohydrate ...27g Saturates 1g

 20 mins   35 mins

SERVES 4

I N G R E D I E N T S

2 tbsp olive oil

500 g/1 lb 2 oz small new potatoes, halved

1 onion, halved and sliced

1 green pepper, deseeded and
  cut into strips

1 tsp chilli powder

1 tsp prepared mustard

300 ml/10 fl oz passata

300 ml/10 fl oz vegetable stock

salt and pepper

chopped parsley, to garnish

1 Heat the olive oil in a large heavy-based frying pan. Add the new potatoes and onion and cook, stirring frequently, for 4–5 minutes, until the onion slices are soft and translucent.

2 Add the green pepper strips, chilli powder and mustard to the pan and cook for a further 2–3 minutes.

3 Stir the passata and the vegetable stock into the pan and bring to the boil. Reduce the heat and simmer for about 25 minutes, or until the potatoes are tender. Season to taste.

4 Transfer the potatoes to a warmed serving dish. Sprinkle the parsley over the top and serve immediately. Alternatively, leave the Spanish potatoes to cool completely and serve cold, at room temperature.

COOK'S TIP

In Spain, *tapas* are traditionally served with a glass of chilled sherry or some other aperitif.

Spicy Indian Potatoes

In Indian cooking there are many variations of spicy potatoes.
In this recipe, spinach is added for both colour and flavour.

NUTRITIONAL INFORMATION

Calories 65   Sugars 1.9g
Protein ....2.5g   Fat 3.4g
Carbohydrate ...6.5g   Saturates 0.4g

10 mins   40 mins

SERVES 4

I N G R E D I E N T S

½ tsp coriander seeds

1 tsp cumin seeds

4 tbsp vegetable oil

2 cardamon pods

1 tsp grated fresh root ginger

1 red chilli, chopped

1 onion, chopped

2 garlic cloves, crushed

450 g/1 lb new potatoes, quartered

150 ml/5 fl oz vegetable stock

675 g/1½ lb spinach, chopped

4 tbsp natural yogurt

salt and pepper

1 Grind the coriander and cumin seeds using a pestle and mortar.

2 Heat the oil in a frying pan. Add the ground coriander and cumin seeds to the pan together with the cardamom pods and ginger and cook for about 2 minutes.

3 Add the chilli, onion and garlic to the pan. Cook for a further 2 minutes, stirring frequently.

4 Add the potatoes to the pan together with the vegetable stock. Cook gently for 30 minutes or until the potatoes are cooked through, stirring occasionally.

5 Add the spinach to the pan and cook for a further 5 minutes.

6 Remove the pan from the heat and stir in the yogurt. Season with salt and pepper to taste. Transfer the potatoes and spinach to a serving dish and serve.

VARIATION

Use frozen spinach instead of fresh spinach, if you prefer. Defrost the frozen spinach and drain it thoroughly before adding it to the dish, otherwise it will turn soggy.

Potatoes in Red Wine

This is a rich recipe that is best served with plain dark meats, such as beef or game, to complement the flavour.

NUTRITIONAL INFORMATION

Calories . . . . .116 Sugars 1.4g
Protein . . . . .1.5g Fat 8.7g
Carbohydrate . . . .7g Saturates 5.7g

  5 mins   45 mins

SERVES 4

I N G R E D I E N T S

125 g/4½ oz butter

450 g/1 lb new potatoes, halved

200 ml/7 fl oz red wine

6 tbsp beef stock

8 shallots, halved

125 g/4½ oz oyster mushrooms

1 tbsp chopped fresh sage or coriander

salt and pepper

sage leaves or coriander sprigs, to garnish

VARIATION

If oyster mushrooms are unavailable, other mushrooms, such as large open cap mushrooms, can be used instead.

1 Melt the butter in a heavy-based frying pan and add the potatoes. Cook gently for 5 minutes, stirring constantly.

2 Add the red wine, beef stock and shallots. Season to taste with salt and pepper and simmer for 30 minutes.

3 Stir in the mushrooms and chopped herbs and cook for 5 minutes.

4 Turn the potatoes and mushrooms into a warm serving dish. Garnish with fresh sage leaves or coriander sprigs and serve at once.

Gingered Potatoes

This simple spicy dish is ideal with a plain main course. The cashew nuts and celery add extra crunch.

NUTRITIONAL INFORMATION

Calories . . . . . . .325 Sugars 1g
Protein . . . . .5g Fat 21g
Carbohydrate . . .30g Saturates 9g

 20 mins   30 mins

SERVES 4

INGREDIENTS

675 g/1½ lb waxy potatoes, cubed

2 tbsp vegetable oil

4 tsp grated fresh root ginger

1 fresh green chilli, chopped

1 celery stick, chopped

25 g/1 oz cashew nuts

few strands of saffron

3 tbsp boiling water

5 tbsp butter

celery leaves, to garnish

1 Cook the potatoes in a saucepan of boiling water for 10 minutes, then drain thoroughly.

2 Heat the oil in a heavy-based frying pan and add the potatoes. Cook over a medium heat, stirring constantly, for about 3–4 minutes.

3 Add the grated ginger, chilli, celery and cashew nuts and cook for another minute.

4 Meanwhile, place the saffron strands in a small bowl. Add the boiling water and set aside to soak for 5 minutes.

5 Add the butter to the pan, lower the heat and stir in the saffron mixture. Cook over a low heat for 10 minutes, or until the potatoes are tender.

6 Transfer to a warm serving dish, garnish the gingered potatoes with the celery leaves and serve at once.

COOK'S TIP

Use a non-stick, heavy-based frying pan because the potato mixture is fairly dry and may stick to an ordinary pan.

Potato Stir-fry

In this sweet and sour dish, tender vegetables are simply stir-fried with spices and coconut milk, and flavoured with lime.

NUTRITIONAL INFORMATION

Calories	138	Sugars	.........5g
Protein	.........2g	Fat	...........6g
Carbohydrate	...20g	Saturates	.......1g

 10 mins   20 mins

SERVES 4

I N G R E D I E N T S

900 g/2 lb waxy potatoes

2 tbsp vegetable oil

1 yellow pepper, diced

1 red pepper, diced

1 carrot, cut into matchsticks

1 courgette, cut into matchsticks

2 garlic cloves, crushed

1 red chilli, sliced

1 bunch spring onions, halved lengthways

125 ml/4 fl oz coconut milk

1 tsp chopped lemon grass

2 tsp lime juice

finely grated rind of 1 lime

1 tbsp chopped fresh coriander

1 Using a sharp knife, cut the potatoes into small cubes.

2 Bring a large saucepan of water to the boil and cook the diced potatoes for 5 minutes. Drain thoroughly.

3 Heat the vegetable oil in a wok or large frying pan, swirling the oil around the base of the wok until it is really hot.

4 Add the potatoes, peppers, carrot, courgette, garlic and chilli to the wok and stir-fry the vegetables for 2–3 minutes.

5 Stir in the spring onions, coconut milk, lemon grass and lime juice and stir-fry the mixture for a further 5 minutes.

6 Add the lime rind and chopped fresh coriander and stir-fry for 1 minute. Serve immediately while hot.

COOK'S TIP
Check that the potatoes are not overcooked in step 2, otherwise the potato pieces will disintegrate when they are stir-fried in the wok.

Cheese & Potato Slices

This recipe takes a while to prepare but it is well worth the effort.
The golden potato slices coated in breadcrumbs and cheese are delicious.

NUTRITIONAL INFORMATION

Calories 560	Sugars 3g
Protein 19g	Fat 31g
Carbohydrate ...55g	Saturates 7g

 10 mins   40 mins

SERVES 4

INGREDIENTS

900 g/2 lb waxy potatoes, unpeeled and
   thickly sliced

70 g/2½ oz fresh white breadcrumbs

40 g/1½ oz Parmesan cheese, freshly
   grated

1½ tsp chilli powder

2 eggs, beaten

oil, for deep frying

chilli powder, for dusting (optional)

1 Cook the potatoes in a saucepan of boiling water for about 10–15 minutes, or until the potatoes are just tender. Drain thoroughly.

2 Mix the breadcrumbs, cheese and chilli powder together in a bowl, then transfer to a shallow dish. Pour the beaten eggs into a separate shallow dish.

3 Dip the potato slices first in egg and then roll them in the breadcrumbs to coat completely.

4 Heat the oil in a large saucepan or deep-fryer to 180°C/350°F or until a cube of bread browns in 30 seconds. Cook the cheese and potato slices, in several batches, for 4–5 minutes or until a golden brown colour.

5 Remove the cheese and potato slices from the oil with a slotted spoon and drain thoroughly on kitchen paper. Keep the cheese and potato slices warm while you cook the remaining batches.

6 Transfer the cheese and potato slices to warm individual serving plates. Dust lightly with chilli powder, if using, and serve immediately.

COOK'S TIP

The cheese and potato slices may be coated in the breadcrumb mixture in advance and then stored in the refrigerator until ready to use.

Grilled Potatoes with Lime

This dish is ideal with grilled or barbecued foods, because the potatoes themselves may be cooked by either method.

NUTRITIONAL INFORMATION

Calories 253   Sugars 0.7g
Protein . . . . .1.8g   Fat 22.2g
Carbohydrate . .12.4g   Saturates 5.8g

 10 mins   15–20 mins

SERVES 4

I N G R E D I E N T S

450 g/1 lb potatoes, unpeeled and scrubbed

3 tbsp butter, melted

2 tbsp chopped fresh thyme

paprika, for dusting

L I M E   M A Y O N N A I S E

150 ml/5 fl oz mayonnaise

2 tsp lime juice

finely grated rind of 1 lime

1 garlic clove, crushed

pinch of paprika

salt and pepper

1 Cut the potatoes into 1-cm/½-inch-thick slices.

2 Cook the potatoes in a saucepan of boiling water for 5–7 minutes – they should still be quite firm. Remove the potatoes with a perforated spoon and drain thoroughly.

3 Line a grill pan with kitchen foil. Place the potato slices on top of the foil.

4 Brush the potatoes with the melted butter and sprinkle the thyme on top. Season to taste with salt and pepper.

5 Cook the potatoes under a preheated medium grill for 10 minutes, turning once during cooking.

6 Meanwhile, make the lime mayonnaise. In a small bowl, combine the mayonnaise, lime juice, lime rind, garlic, paprika and season with salt and pepper to taste.

7 Dust the hot potato slices with a little paprika and serve them with the lime mayonnaise.

COOK'S TIP
For an impressive side dish, thread the potato slices on to skewers and cook over medium-hot barbecue coals.

Trio of Potato Purées

These small moulds filled with layers of flavoured potato look very impressive. They are ideal with fish or roast meats.

NUTRITIONAL INFORMATION

Calories . . . . 170 Sugars 5g
Protein . . . . 7g Fat 6g
Carbohydrate . . . 24g Saturates 3g

 15 mins   1 hr 15 mins

SERVES 4

I N G R E D I E N T S

300 g/10½ oz floury potatoes, chopped

125 g/4½ oz swede, chopped

1 carrot, chopped

450 g/1 lb spinach

1 tbsp skimmed milk

1 tbsp butter

2½ tbsp plain flour

1 egg

½ tsp ground cinnamon

1 tbsp orange juice

¼ tsp grated nutmeg

salt and pepper

carrot matchsticks, to garnish

1 Lightly grease four 150 ml/5 fl oz ramekins.

2 Cook the potatoes in a saucepan of boiling water for 10 minutes. In separate pans cook the swede and carrot in boiling water for 10 minutes. Blanch the spinach in boiling water for 5 minutes. Drain the vegetables. Add the milk and butter to the potatoes and mash until smooth. Stir in the flour and egg.

3 Divide the potato mixture into three bowls. Spoon the swede into one bowl and mix well. Spoon the carrot into the second bowl and mix well. Spoon the spinach into the third bowl and mix well.

4 Add the cinnamon to the swede and potato mixture and season to taste. Stir the orange juice into the carrot and potato mixture. Stir the nutmeg into the spinach and potato mixture.

5 Spoon a layer of the swede and potato mixture into each of the ramekins and smooth over the top. Cover each with a layer of spinach and potato mixture, then top with the carrot and potato mixture. Cover the ramekins with kitchen foil and place in a roasting tin. Half fill the tin with boiling water and cook in a preheated oven, 180°C/350°F/Gas Mark 4, for 40 minutes or until set.

6 Turn out on to serving plates, garnish with the carrot matchsticks and serve immediately.

Spicy Potato Fries

These home-made chips are flavoured with spices and cooked in the oven. Serve with Lime Mayonnaise (see page 123).

NUTRITIONAL INFORMATION

Calories ....328 Sugars 2g
Protein ....5g Fat 11g
Carbohydrate ...56g Saturates 7g

15 mins, plus 20 mins soaking time

40 mins

SERVES 4

INGREDIENTS

4 large waxy potatoes

2 sweet potatoes

4 tbsp butter, melted

½ tsp chilli powder

1 tsp garam masala

salt

1 Cut the potatoes and sweet potatoes into slices about 1 cm/½ inch thick, then cut them into chip shapes.

2 Place the potatoes in a large bowl of cold salted water. Set aside to soak for 20 minutes.

3 Remove the potato slices with a slotted spoon and drain thoroughly. Pat with kitchen paper until they are completely dry.

 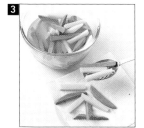 

COOK'S TIP

Rinsing the potatoes in cold water before cooking removes the starch, thus preventing them from sticking together. Soaking the potatoes in a bowl of cold salted water actually makes the cooked chips crisper.

4 Pour the melted butter on to a baking tray. Transfer the potato slices to the baking tray.

5 Sprinkle with the chilli powder and garam masala, turning the potato slices to coat them with the mixture.

6 Cook the chips in a preheated oven, 200°C/400°F/Gas Mark 6, turning frequently, for 40 minutes, until browned and cooked through.

7 Drain the chips on kitchen paper to remove the excess oil and serve.

Italian Potato Wedges

These oven-cooked potato wedges use classic pizza ingredients and are delicious served with plain meats, such as pork or lamb.

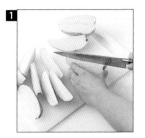

NUTRITIONAL INFORMATION

Calories	115	Sugars 4g
Protein	.........6g	Fat 5g
Carbohydrate	...13g	Saturates 3g

15 mins   35 mins

SERVES 4

I N G R E D I E N T S

2 large waxy potatoes, unpeeled

4 large ripe tomatoes, peeled and deseeded

150 ml/5 fl oz vegetable stock

2 tbsp tomato purée

1 small yellow pepper, cut into strips

125 g/4 ½ oz button mushrooms, quartered

1 tbsp chopped fresh basil

50 g/1 ¾ oz cheese, grated

salt and pepper

1 Cut each of the potatoes into 8 equal wedges. Parboil the potatoes in a pan of boiling water for 15 minutes. Drain well and place in a shallow ovenproof dish.

2 Chop the tomatoes and add to the dish. Mix together the vegetable stock and tomato purée, then pour the mixture over the potatoes and tomatoes.

3 Add the yellow pepper strips, mushrooms and basil. Season well with salt and pepper.

4 Sprinkle the grated cheese over the top and cook in a preheated oven, 190°C/375°F/Gas Mark 5, for 15–20 minutes until the topping is golden brown. Serve at once.

Saffron-flavoured Potatoes

Saffron is made from the dried stigma of the crocus and is native to Greece. It is very expensive, but only a very small amount is needed.

NUTRITIONAL INFORMATION

Calories	197	Sugars	.........4g
Protein	.........4g	Fat	...........6g
Carbohydrate	...30g	Saturates	.......1g

 20 mins   40 mins

SERVES 4

INGREDIENTS

1 tsp saffron strands

6 tbsp boiling water

675 g/1½ lb waxy potatoes,
    unpeeled and cut into wedges

1 red onion, cut into 8 wedges

2 garlic cloves, crushed

1 tbsp white wine vinegar

2 tbsp olive oil

1 tbsp wholegrain mustard

5 tbsp vegetable stock

5 tbsp dry white wine

2 tsp chopped fresh rosemary

salt and pepper

1 Place the saffron strands in a small bowl and pour over the boiling water. Set aside to soak for about 10 minutes.

2 Place the potatoes in a roasting tin, together with the red onion and the garlic.

3 Add the vinegar, oil, mustard, vegetable stock, white wine, rosemary and saffron water to the potatoes and onion in the tin. Season to taste with salt and pepper.

4 Cover the roasting tin with kitchen foil and bake in a preheated oven, 200°C/400°F/Gas Mark 6, for 30 minutes.

5 Remove the foil and cook the potatoes for a further 10 minutes until crisp, browned and cooked through. Serve hot.

COOK'S TIP
Turmeric may be used instead of saffron to provide the yellow colour in this recipe. However, it is worth using saffron, if possible, for the lovely nutty flavour it gives a dish.

Chilli Roast Potatoes

Small new potatoes are scrubbed and boiled in their skins, before being coated in a chilli mixture and roasted to perfection in the oven.

NUTRITIONAL INFORMATION

Calories	178	Sugars	.........2g
Protein	.........2g	Fat	...........11g
Carbohydrate	...18g	Saturates	.......1g

  5–10 mins   30 mins

SERVES 4

INGREDIENTS

500 g/1 lb 2 oz small new potatoes, scrubbed

150 ml/5 fl oz vegetable oil

1 tsp chilli powder

½ tsp caraway seeds

1 tsp salt

1 tbsp chopped basil

1 Cook the potatoes in a saucepan of boiling water for 10 minutes, then drain thoroughly.

2 Pour a little of the oil into a shallow roasting tin to coat the base. Heat the oil in a preheated oven, 200°C/ 400°F/Gas Mark 6, for 10 minutes. Add the potatoes to the tin and brush them with the hot oil.

3 In a small bowl, mix together the chilli powder, caraway seeds and salt. Sprinkle the mixture over the potatoes, turning to coat them all over.

4 Add the remaining oil to the tin and roast in the oven for about 15 minutes, or until the potatoes are cooked through.

5 Using a slotted spoon, remove the potatoes from the the oil, draining them well, and transfer them to a warmed serving dish. Sprinkle the chopped basil over the top and serve immediately.

VARIATION

Use any other spice of your choice, such as curry powder or paprika, for a variation in flavour.

Parmesan Potatoes

This is a very simple way to jazz up roast potatoes. Serve them in the same way as roast potatoes with roasted meats or fish.

NUTRITIONAL INFORMATION

Calories	307	Sugars	.........2g
Protein	........11g	Fat	..........14g
Carbohydrate	...37g	Saturates	.......6g

 15 mins   1 hr 5 mins

SERVES 4

INGREDIENTS

1.3 kg/3 lb potatoes

50 g/1 ¾ oz Parmesan cheese, freshly grated

pinch of grated nutmeg

1 tbsp chopped fresh parsley

4 smoked bacon slices, cut into strips

vegetable oil, for roasting

salt

1 Cut the potatoes in half lengthways and cook them in a saucepan of boiling salted water for 10 minutes. Drain thoroughly.

2 Mix the grated Parmesan cheese, nutmeg and parsley together in a shallow bowl.

3 Roll the potato pieces in the cheese mixture to coat them completely. Shake off any excess.

4 Pour a little oil into a roasting tin and then heat it in a preheated oven, 200°C/400°F/Gas Mark 6, for 10 minutes. Remove from the oven and put the potatoes into the tin. Return the potatoes to the oven and cook for 30 minutes, turning once.

5 Remove from the oven and sprinkle the bacon on top of the potatoes. Return to the oven for 15 minutes or until the potatoes and bacon are cooked. Drain off any excess fat and serve.

VARIATION

If you prefer, use slices of salami or Parma ham instead of the bacon, adding it to the dish 5 minutes before the end of the cooking time.

Potatoes with Almonds

This oven-cooked dish has a subtle, creamy almond flavour and a pale yellow colour as a result of being cooked with turmeric.

NUTRITIONAL INFORMATION

Calories . . . . .531 Sugars 6g
Protein . . . . .7g Fat 46g
Carbohydrate . . .24g Saturates 23g

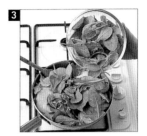 

 5 mins   40–45 mins

SERVES 4

I N G R E D I E N T S

600 g/1 lb 5 oz potatoes, unpeeled and sliced

1 tbsp vegetable oil

1 red onion, halved and sliced

1 garlic clove, crushed

50 g/1¾ oz almond flakes

½ tsp turmeric

125 g/4½ oz rocket leaves

300ml/10 fl oz double cream

salt and pepper

1 Cook the sliced potatoes in a saucepan of boiling water for 10 minutes. Drain thoroughly.

2 Heat the vegetable oil in a heavy-based frying pan. Add the onion and garlic and fry over a medium heat, stirring frequently, for 3–4 minutes.

3 Add the almonds, turmeric and potato slices to the frying pan and cook, stirring constantly, for 2–3 minutes. Stir in the rocket.

4 Transfer the potato and almond mixture to a shallow ovenproof dish. Pour the double cream over the top and season with salt and pepper.

5 Cook in a preheated oven, 190°C/ 375°F/Gas Mark 5, for 20 minutes, or until the potatoes are cooked through. Transfer to a warmed serving dish and serve immediately.

Spicy Potatoes & Onions

Masala aloo are potatoes cooked in a spicy mixture called baghaar. When cooked semi-dry, they make an excellent accompaniment to a curry.

NUTRITIONAL INFORMATION

Calories 313   Sugars 5g
Protein . . . . .2g   Fat 25g
Carbohydrate . . .21g   Saturates 3g

  10–15 mins   10 mins

SERVES 4

I N G R E D I E N T S

6 tbsp vegetable oil

2 onions, finely chopped

1 tsp finely chopped fresh root ginger

1 tsp crushed garlic

1 tsp chilli powder

1½ tsp ground cumin

1½ tsp ground coriander

1 tsp salt

400 g/14 oz canned new potatoes

1 tbsp lemon juice

B A G H A A R

3 tbsp oil

3 dried red chillies

½ tsp onion seeds

½ tsp mustard seeds

½ tsp fenugreek seeds

T O   G A R N I S H

fresh coriander leaves

1 green chilli, finely chopped

ground cumin, ground coriander and salt and stir-fry for about 1 minute. Remove the pan from the heat and set aside until required.

1 Heat the oil in a large, heavy-based saucepan. Add the onions and fry, stirring, until golden brown. Reduce the heat, add the ginger, garlic, chilli powder,

2 Drain the water from the potatoes. Add the potatoes to the onion and spice mixture and heat through. Sprinkle over the lemon juice and mix well.

3 To make the baghaar, heat the oil in a separate pan. Add the red chillies, onion seeds, mustard seeds and fenugreek seeds and fry until the seeds turn a shade darker. Remove the pan from the heat and pour the baghaar over the potatoes.

4 Garnish with coriander leaves and chillies, then serve.

Cheese & Potato Pie

This really is a great side dish, perfect for serving alongside main meals cooked in the oven.

NUTRITIONAL INFORMATION

Calories 295	Sugars 5g	
Protein 13g	Fat 17g	
Carbohydrate ...24g	Saturates 11g	

 15 mins   1 hr 30 mins

SERVES 4

INGREDIENTS

500 g/1 lb 2 oz potatoes

1 leek, sliced

3 garlic cloves, crushed

50 g/1¾ oz Cheddar cheese, grated

50 g/1¾ oz mozzarella cheese, grated

25 g/1 oz Parmesan cheese, freshly grated

2 tbsp chopped parsley

150 ml/5 fl oz single cream

150 ml/5 fl oz milk

salt and pepper

chopped flat leaf parsley, to garnish

1 Cook the potatoes in a saucepan of boiling salted water for 10 minutes. Drain well.

2 Cut the potatoes into thin slices. Arrange a layer of potatoes in the base of an ovenproof dish. Layer with a little of the leek, garlic, cheeses and parsley. Season to taste.

3 Repeat the layers until all of the ingredients have been used, finishing with a layer of cheese. Mix the cream and milk together, season with salt and pepper to taste and pour over the potato layers.

4 Cook in a preheated oven, 160°C/325°F/Gas Mark 3, for 1–1¼ hours, or until the cheese is golden brown and bubbling and the potatoes are cooked through and tender.

5 Garnish with chopped fresh flat leaf parsley and serve immediately.

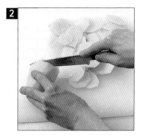

COOK'S TIP

Potatoes make a very good basis for a vegetable accompaniment. They are a good source of complex carbohydrate and contain a number of vitamins. From the point of view of flavour, they combine well with a vast range of other ingredients.

Spiced Potatoes & Spinach

This is a classic Indian accompaniment for many different curries or plainer main vegetable dishes. It is very quick to cook.

NUTRITIONAL INFORMATION

Calories 176   Sugars 4g
Protein ....6g   Fat 9g
Carbohydrate ...18g   Saturates 1g

 10 mins   20 mins

SERVES 4

INGREDIENTS

3 tbsp vegetable oil

1 red onion, sliced

2 garlic cloves, crushed

½ tsp chilli powder

2 tsp ground coriander

1 tsp ground cumin

150 ml/5 fl oz vegetable stock

300 g/10½ oz potatoes, diced

500 g/1 lb 2 oz baby spinach

1 red chilli, sliced

salt and pepper

1 Heat the oil in a heavy-based frying pan. Add the onion and garlic and sauté over a medium heat, stirring occasionally, for 2–3 minutes.

2 Stir in the chilli powder, ground coriander and cumin and cook, stirring constantly, for a further 30 seconds.

3 Add the vegetable stock, potatoes and spinach and bring to the boil. Reduce the heat, cover the frying pan and simmer for about 10 minutes, or until the potatoes are cooked through and tender.

4 Uncover, season to taste with salt and pepper, add the chilli and cook for a further 2–3 minutes. Transfer to a warmed serving dish and serve immediately.

COOK'S TIP

Besides adding extra colour to a dish, red onions have a sweeter, less pungent flavour than other varieties.

Souffléd Cheesy Potato Fries

These small potato chunks are mixed in a creamy cheese sauce and fried in oil until deliciously golden brown.

NUTRITIONAL INFORMATION

Calories . . . . .614 Sugars 2g
Protein . . . . .12g Fat 46g
Carbohydrate . . .40g Saturates 18g

 20 mins   25 mins

SERVES 4

I N G R E D I E N T S

900 g/2 lb potatoes, cut into chunks

150 ml/5 fl oz double cream

75 g/2¾ oz Gruyère cheese, grated

pinch of cayenne pepper

2 egg whites

vegetable oil, for deep-frying

salt and pepper

TO GARNISH

chopped flat leaf parsley

grated cheese

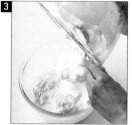

1 Cook the potatoes in a saucepan of lightly salted boiling water for about 10 minutes. Drain thoroughly and pat dry with absorbent kitchen paper. Set aside until required.

2 Mix the double cream and Gruyère cheese in a large bowl. Stir in the cayenne pepper and season with salt and pepper to taste.

3 Whisk the egg whites until stiff peaks form. Gently fold into the cheese mixture until fully incorporated.

4 Add the cooked potatoes, turning to coat thoroughly in the mixture.

5 Heat the oil for deep-frying to 180°C/350°F or until a cube of bread browns in 30 seconds. Remove the potatoes from the cheese mixture with a slotted spoon and cook in the oil, in batches if necessary, for 3–4 minutes, or until golden.

6 Transfer the potatoes to a warmed serving dish and garnish with parsley and grated cheese. Serve immediately.

VARIATION
Add other flavourings, such as grated nutmeg or curry powder, to the cream and cheese.

Pesto Potatoes

Pesto sauce is more commonly used as a pasta sauce but is also delicious served over potatoes.

NUTRITIONAL INFORMATION

Calories 531   Sugars 3g
Protein . . . . .13g   Fat 38g
Carbohydrate . . .36g   Saturates 8g

 15 mins   15 mins

SERVES 4

INGREDIENTS

900 g/2 lb small new potatoes

75 g/2¾ oz fresh basil

2 tbsp pine kernels

3 garlic cloves, crushed

100 ml/3½ fl oz olive oil

75 g/2¾ oz mixed Parmesan cheese and pecorino cheese, grated

salt and pepper

fresh basil sprigs, to garnish

1 Cook the potatoes in a saucepan of boiling salted water for 15 minutes or until tender. Drain well, transfer to a warm serving dish and keep warm until required.

2 Meanwhile, put the basil, pine kernels, garlic and a little salt and pepper to taste in a food processor. Blend for 30 seconds, adding the oil gradually, until smooth.

3 Remove the mixture from the food processor and transfer it to a mixing bowl. Stir in the grated Parmesan and Pecorino cheeses.

4 Spoon the pesto sauce over the potatoes and mix well. Garnish with fresh basil sprigs and serve immediately.

Mini Vegetable Puff Pastries

These puff pastries are ideal with a more formal meal because they take a short time to prepare and look really impressive.

NUTRITIONAL INFORMATION

Calories 210	Sugars 2.3g
Protein 3.8g	Fat 12.9g
Carbohydrate . .20.8g	Saturates 1.7g

15 mins   25 mins

SERVES 4

INGREDIENTS

PASTRY CASES

450 g/1 lb puff pastry

1 egg, beaten

FILLING

225 g/8 oz sweet potatoes, cubed

100 g/3½ oz baby asparagus spears

2 tbsp butter or margarine

1 leek, sliced

2 small open-cap mushrooms, sliced

1 tsp lime juice

1 tsp chopped fresh thyme

pinch of dried mustard

salt and pepper

  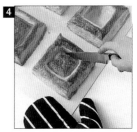

1 Cut the pastry into 4 equal pieces. Roll each piece out on a lightly floured work surface to form a 13-cm/5-inch square. Place on a dampened baking tray and score a smaller 6-cm/2½-inch square inside.

2 Brush with beaten egg and cook in a preheated oven, 200°C/400°F/Gas Mark 6, for 20 minutes or until risen and golden brown.

3 While the pastry is cooking, start the filling. Cook the sweet potato in boiling water for 15 minutes, then drain.

Blanch the asparagus in boiling water for 10 minutes or until tender. Drain and reserve.

4 Remove the pastry squares from the oven. Carefully cut out the central square of pastry, lift it out and reserve.

5 Melt the butter or margarine in a pan and sauté the leek and mushrooms for 2–3 minutes. Add the lime juice, thyme and mustard, season well and stir in the sweet potatoes and asparagus. Spoon into the pastry cases, top with the reserved pastry squares and serve immediately.

COOK'S TIP

Use a colourful selection of any vegetables you have at hand for this recipe.

Bombay Potatoes

Although virtually unknown in India, this dish is a very popular item on Indian restaurant menus in other parts of the world.

NUTRITIONAL INFORMATION

Calories 307	Sugars 9g
Protein 9g	Fat 9g
Carbohydrate . . .51g	Saturates 5g

 5 mins   1 hr 10 mins

SERVES 4

I N G R E D I E N T S

1 kg/2 lb 4 oz waxy potatoes

2 tbsp vegetable ghee

1 tsp panch poran spice mix

3 tsp ground turmeric

2 tbsp tomato purée

300 ml/10 fl oz natural yogurt

salt

chopped fresh coriander, to garnish

1 Put the whole potatoes into a large saucepan of salted cold water, bring to the boil, then simmer until the potatoes are just cooked, but not tender; the time depends on the size of the potato, but an average-sized one should take about 15 minutes.

COOK'S TIP

Panch poran spice mix can be bought from Asian or Indian grocery stores, or make your own from equal quantities of cumin seeds, fennel seeds, mustard seeds, nigella seeds and fenugreek seeds.

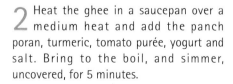

2 Heat the ghee in a saucepan over a medium heat and add the panch poran, turmeric, tomato purée, yogurt and salt. Bring to the boil, and simmer, uncovered, for 5 minutes.

3 Drain the potatoes and cut each one into 4 pieces. Add the potatoes to the pan, cover and cook briefly. Transfer to an ovenproof casserole, cover and cook in a preheated oven, 180°C/350°F/Gas Mark 4, for about 40 minutes, or until the potatoes are tender and the sauce has thickened a little.

4 Sprinkle with chopped coriander and serve immediately.

Potato Salad

You can use leftover cold potatoes, cut into bite-size pieces, for this salad, but tiny new potatoes are best for maximum flavour.

NUTRITIONAL INFORMATION

Calories . . . . . . .275 Sugars 8g
Protein . . . . .5g Fat 13g
Carbohydrate . . .38g Saturates 2g

   20 mins   10–15 mins

SERVES 4

I N G R E D I E N T S

700 g/1 lb 9 oz tiny new potatoes

8 spring onions

1 hard-boiled egg, optional

250 ml/9 fl oz low-fat mayonnaise

1 tsp paprika

salt and pepper

T O   G A R N I S H

2 tbsp snipped chives

pinch of paprika

1 Bring a large pan of lightly salted water to the boil. Add the potatoes to the pan and cook for 10–15 minutes or until they are just tender.

2 Drain the potatoes in a colander and rinse them under cold running water until they are completely cold. Drain them

again thoroughly. Transfer the potatoes to a mixing bowl and set aside until required.

3 Trim and slice the spring onions thinly on the diagonal. Chop the hard-boiled egg (if using).

4 Mix together the mayonnaise, paprika and salt and pepper to taste in a bowl until well blended. Pour the mixture over the potatoes.

5 Add the sliced spring onions and egg (if using) to the potatoes and toss together.

6 Transfer the potato salad to a serving bowl, sprinkle with snipped chives and a pinch of paprika. Cover and leave to chill in the refrigerator until required.

COOK'S TIP

To make a lighter dressing, use a mixture of half mayonnaise and half natural yogurt.

Potatoes Lyonnaise

In this classic French recipe, sliced potatoes are cooked with onions to make a delicious accompaniment to a main meal.

NUTRITIONAL INFORMATION

Calories 277	Sugars 4g	
Protein 5g	Fat 12g	
Carbohydrate ...40g	Saturates 4g	

 10 mins   25 mins

SERVES 6

INGREDIENTS

1.25 kg/2 lb 12 oz potatoes

4 tbsp olive oil

2 tbsp butter

2 onions, sliced

2–3 garlic cloves, crushed (optional)

salt and pepper

chopped parsley, to garnish

1 Cut the potatoes into 5-mm/¼-inch slices. Put in a large saucepan of lightly salted water and bring to the boil. Cover and simmer gently for about 10–12 minutes, until just tender. Avoid boiling too rapidly or the potatoes will break up and lose their shape. When cooked, drain well.

COOK'S TIP
If the potatoes blacken slightly as they are boiling, add a spoonful of lemon juice to the cooking water.

2 While the potatoes are cooking, heat the oil and butter in a very large frying pan. Add the onions and garlic, if using, and fry over a medium heat, stirring frequently, until the onions are softened.

3 Add the cooked potato to the frying pan and cook with the onions, stirring occasionally, for about 5–8 minutes until the potatoes are well browned.

4 Season to taste with salt and pepper. Sprinkle over the chopped parsley to serve. If wished, transfer the potatoes and onions to a large ovenproof dish and keep warm in a low oven until ready to serve.

Vegetarian & Vegan Suppers

The potato has become a valued staple of the vegetarian diet, yet anyone who thought this would make for dull eating will be pleasantly surprised by the rich variety of dishes in this chapter. In addition to traditional hearty bakes and hotpots, there are also influences from around the world in dishes such as Tofu & Vegetable Stir-fry from China, and Potato & Cauliflower Curry from India. They all make exciting eating at any time of year.

Mixed Bean Soup

This is a really hearty soup, filled with colour, flavour and goodness, which may be adapted to any vegetables that you have at hand.

NUTRITIONAL INFORMATION

Calories	190	Sugars	.........9g
Protein	........10g	Fat	..........4g
Carbohydrate	...30g	Saturates	.....0.5g

 10 mins   40 mins

SERVES 4

INGREDIENTS

1 tbsp vegetable oil

1 red onion, halved and sliced

100 g/3½ oz potatoes, diced

1 carrot, diced

1 leek, sliced

1 green chilli, sliced

3 garlic cloves, crushed

1 tsp ground coriander

1 tsp chilli powder

1 litre/1¾ pints vegetable stock

450 g/1 lb mixed canned beans, such as red kidney, borlotti, black eye or flageolet, drained

salt and pepper

2 tbsp chopped fresh coriander, to garnish

1 Heat the vegetable oil in a large saucepan. Add the onion, potatoes, carrot and leek and sauté, stirring constantly, for about 2 minutes, until the vegetables are slightly softened.

2 Add the chilli and crushed garlic and cook for a further minute.

3 Stir in the ground coriander, chilli powder and vegetable stock.

4 Bring the soup to the boil, reduce the heat and cook for 20 minutes, or until the vegetables are tender.

5 Stir in the beans, season well with salt and pepper and cook, stirring occasionally, for a further 10 minutes.

6 Transfer the soup to a warm tureen or individual bowls, garnish with chopped coriander and serve.

COOK'S TIP

Serve this soup with slices of warm corn bread or a cheese loaf.

Pepper & Mushroom Hash

This quick one-pan dish is ideal for a snack. Packed with colour and flavour, it is very versatile because you can add other vegetables.

NUTRITIONAL INFORMATION

Calories 182   Sugars 6g
Protein ....5g   Fat 4g
Carbohydrate ...34g   Saturates 0.5g

 5 mins   30 mins

SERVES 4

INGREDIENTS

675 g/1½ lb potatoes, cubed

1 tbsp olive oil

2 garlic cloves, crushed

1 green pepper, deseeded
    and cubed

1 yellow pepper, deseeded
    and cubed

3 tomatoes, diced

75 g/2¾ oz button mushrooms, halved

1 tbsp Worcestershire sauce

2 tbsp chopped fresh basil

salt and pepper

basil leaves, to garnish

warm crusty bread, to serve

1 Cook the potatoes in a saucepan of boiling salted water for 7–8 minutes. Drain well and reserve.

2 Heat the olive oil in a large, heavy-based frying pan. Add the potatoes and cook, stirring constantly, for 8–10 minutes, until browned.

3 Add the garlic and peppers and cook, stirring frequently, for 2–3 minutes.

4 Stir in the tomatoes and mushrooms and cook, stirring frequently, for 5–6 minutes.

5 Stir in the Worcestershire sauce and basil and season to taste with salt and pepper. Transfer to a warm serving dish, garnish with basil sprigs and serve with warm crusty bread.

COOK'S TIP

Most brands of Worcestershire sauce contain anchovies, so if you are a vegetarian check the label to make sure you choose a vegetarian variety.

Curry Pasties

These pasties, which are suitable for vegans, are a delicious combination of vegetables and spices. They can be eaten either hot or cold.

NUTRITIONAL INFORMATION

Calories	455	Sugars	.........5g
Protein	.........8g	Fat	..........27g
Carbohydrate	...48g	Saturates	.......5g

20 mins, plus 30 mins chilling time   1 hr

SERVES 4

I N G R E D I E N T S

225 g/8 oz plain wholemeal flour

100 g/3½ oz margarine, cut into small pieces

4 tbsp water

2 tbsp vegetable oil

225 g/8 oz diced root vegetables, such as potatoes, carrots and parsnips

1 small onion, chopped

2 garlic cloves, finely chopped

½ tsp curry powder

½ tsp ground turmeric

½ tsp ground cumin

½ tsp wholegrain mustard

5 tbsp vegetable stock

soya milk, to glaze

1 Place the flour in a mixing bowl and rub in the margarine with your fingertips until the mixture resembles breadcrumbs. Stir in the water and bring together to form a soft dough. Wrap and set aside to chill in the refrigerator for 30 minutes.

2 To make the filling, heat the oil in a large saucepan. Add the diced root vegetables, chopped onion and garlic and fry, stirring occasionally, for 2 minutes. Stir in all of the spices, turning the vegetables to coat them thoroughly. Fry the vegetables, stirring constantly, for a further minute.

3 Add the stock to the pan and bring to the boil. Cover and simmer, stirring occasionally, for about 20 minutes, until the vegetables are tender and the liquid has been absorbed. Leave to cool.

4 Divide the pastry into four portions. Roll each portion into a 15-cm/ 6-inch round. Place the filling on one half of each round.

5 Brush the edges of each round with soya milk, then fold over and press the edges together to seal. Place on a baking tray. Bake in a preheated oven, 200°C/ 400°F/Gas Mark 6, for 25–30 minutes until golden brown.

Potato & Vegetable Curry

Very little meat is eaten in India, and the Indian diet is mainly vegetarian.
This potato curry with added vegetables makes a substantial main meal.

NUTRITIONAL INFORMATION

Calories 301   Sugars 10g
Protein . . . . .9g   Fat 12g
Carbohydrate . . .41g   Saturates 1g

  5 mins   45 mins

SERVES 4

INGREDIENTS

4 tbsp vegetable oil

675 g/1½ lb waxy potatoes,
   cut into large chunks

2 onions, quartered

3 garlic cloves, crushed

1 tsp garam masala

½ tsp turmeric

½ tsp ground cumin

½ tsp ground coriander

2 tsp grated fresh root ginger

1 fresh red chilli, chopped

225 g/8 oz cauliflower florets

4 tomatoes, peeled and quartered

75 g/2¾ oz frozen peas

2 tbsp chopped fresh coriander

300 ml10 fl oz vegetable stock

shredded coriander, to garnish

COOK'S TIP

Use a large heavy-based
saucepan or frying pan for this
recipe to ensure that the potatoes
are cooked thoroughly.

1 Heat the vegetable oil in a large heavy-based saucepan or frying pan. Add the potato chunks, onions and garlic and fry over a low heat, stirring frequently, for 2–3 minutes.

2 Add the garam masala, turmeric, ground cumin, ground coriander, ginger and chilli to the pan, mixing the spices into the vegetables. Fry over a low heat, stirring constantly, for 1 minute.

3 Add the cauliflower florets, tomatoes, peas, chopped coriander and vegetable stock to the curry mixture.

4 Cook the potato curry over a low heat for 30–40 minutes, or until the potatoes are tender and completely cooked through.

5 Garnish the potato curry with fresh coriander and serve with plain boiled rice or warm Indian bread.

Green Bean & Potato Curry

You can use fresh or canned green beans for this semi-dry vegetable curry. Serve with dhaal for a good contrast of flavours and colours.

NUTRITIONAL INFORMATION

Calories . . . . . . .690 Sugars 4g
Protein . . . . .3g Fat 69g
Carbohydrate . . .16g Saturates 7g

  15 mins   30 mins

SERVES 4

I N G R E D I E N T S

300 ml/10 fl oz vegetable oil

1 tsp white cumin seeds

1 tsp mustard and onion seeds

4 dried red chillies

3 fresh tomatoes, sliced

1 tsp salt

1 tsp finely chopped fresh root ginger

1 tsp fresh garlic, crushed

1 tsp chilli powder

200 g/7 oz green beans, chopped

450 g/1 lb potatoes, diced

300 ml/10 fl oz water

TO GARNISH

1 tbsp chopped fresh coriander

2 green chillies, finely chopped

COOK'S TIP

Mustard seeds are often fried in oil or ghee to bring out their flavour before being combined with other ingredients.

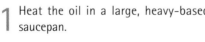

1 Heat the oil in a large, heavy-based saucepan.

2 Add the white cumin seeds, mustard and onion seeds and dried red chillies to the saucepan, stirring well.

3 Add the tomatoes to the pan and stir-fry the mixture for 3-5 minutes.

4 Mix together the salt, ginger, garlic and chilli powder and spoon into the pan. Blend the whole mixture together.

5 Add the green beans and potatoes to the pan and stir-fry for about 5 minutes.

6 Add the water to the pan, reduce the heat and leave to simmer for 10–15 minutes, stirring occasionally.

7 Garnish the green bean and potato curry with chopped coriander leaves and green chillies and serve hot with cooked rice.

Vegetable Kebabs

These kebabs, made from a spicy vegetable mixture, are delightfully easy to make and taste delicious.

NUTRITIONAL INFORMATION

Calories 268	Sugars 1g	
Protein 2g	Fat 25g	
Carbohydrate 9g	Saturates 3g	

  🄖 🄖

🥘 20 mins 🕐 25 mins

MAKES 12

I N G R E D I E N T S

600 g/1 lb 5 oz potatoes, sliced

1 medium onion, sliced

½ medium cauliflower, cut into
small florets

50 g/1¾ oz cooked peas

1 tbsp spinach purée

2–3 green chillies

1 tbsp fresh coriander leaves

1 tsp finely chopped fresh root ginger

1 tsp crushed garlic

1 tsp ground coriander

1 pinch turmeric

1 tsp salt

50 g/1¾ oz breadcrumbs

300 ml/10 fl oz vegetable oil

fresh chilli strips, to garnish

1 Place the potatoes, onion and cauliflower florets in a pan of water and bring to the boil. Reduce the heat and simmer until the potatoes are cooked through. Remove the vegetables from the pan with a slotted spoon and drain thoroughly. Set aside.

2 Add the peas and spinach to the vegetables and mix, mashing down thoroughly with a fork.

3 Using a sharp knife, finely chop the green chillies and the fresh coriander leaves.

4 Mix the chillies and fresh coriander leaves with the ginger, garlic, ground coriander, turmeric and salt.

5 Blend the spice mixture into the vegetables, mixing with a fork to make a paste.

6 Scatter the breadcrumbs on to a large plate.

7 Break off 10–12 small balls from the spice paste. Flatten them with the palm of your hand or with a palette knife to make flat, round shapes.

8 Dip each kebab in the breadcrumbs, coating well.

9 Heat the oil in a heavy-based frying-pan and shallow-fry the kebabs, in batches, until golden brown, turning occasionally. Transfer to serving plates and garnish with fresh chilli strips. Serve hot.

Vegetable Curry

This colourful and interesting mixture of vegetables, cooked in a spicy sauce, is excellent served with rice and naan bread.

NUTRITIONAL INFORMATION

Calories	.421	Sugars	.20g
Protein	.12g	Fat	.24g
Carbohydrate	.42g	Saturates	.3g

10 mins   45 mins

SERVES 4

I N G R E D I E N T S

225 g/8 oz turnips or swede

1 aubergine

350 g/12 oz new potatoes

225 g/8 oz cauliflower

225 g/8 oz button mushrooms

1 large onion

3 carrots

6 tbsp vegetable ghee or oil

2 garlic cloves, crushed

4 tsp finely chopped fresh root ginger

1–2 fresh green chillies, seeded and chopped

1 tbsp paprika

2 tsp ground coriander

1 tbsp mild or medium curry powder or paste

450 ml/16 fl oz vegetable stock

400 g/14 oz canned chopped tomatoes

1 green pepper, deseeded and sliced

1 tbsp cornflour

150 ml/5 fl oz coconut milk

2–3 tbsp ground almonds

salt

coriander sprigs, to garnish

1 Cut the turnips or swede, aubergine and potatoes into 1-cm/½-inch cubes. Divide the cauliflower into small florets. Leave the mushrooms whole, or slice thickly if preferred. Peel and slice the onion and carrots.

2 Heat the ghee or oil in a large saucepan. Add the onion, turnip or swede, potato and cauliflower and cook over a low heat, stirring frequently, for 3 minutes.

3 Add the garlic, ginger, chillies, paprika, ground coriander and curry powder or paste and cook, stirring, for 1 minute.

4 Add the stock, tomatoes, aubergine and mushrooms and season with salt. Cover and simmer, stirring occasionally, for about 30 minutes, or until tender. Add the green pepper and carrots, cover and continue cooking for a further 5 minutes.

5 Blend the cornflour with the coconut milk to a smooth paste and stir into the mixture. Add the ground almonds and simmer, stirring constantly, for 2 minutes. Season if necessary. Transfer the curry to serving plates and serve hot, garnished with sprigs of fresh coriander.

Stuffed Rice Pancakes

Dosas (pancakes) are widely eaten in southern India. The rice and urid dhal need to soak and ferment, so prepare well in advance.

NUTRITIONAL INFORMATION

Calories ....748 Sugars 1g
Protein ....10g Fat 47g
Carbohydrate ...76g Saturates 5g

15 mins, plus
6 hrs soaking/
fermentation

40–45 mins

SERVES 4

INGREDIENTS

200 g/7 oz rice and 50 g/1¾ oz urid dhal, or 200 g/7 oz ground rice and 50 g/1¾ oz urid dhal flour (ata)

425–600 ml/15 fl oz–1 pint water

1 tsp salt

4 tbsp vegetable oil

FILLING

900 g/2 lb potatoes, diced

3 fresh green chillies, chopped

½ tsp turmeric

1 tsp salt

150 ml/5 fl oz vegetable oil

1 tsp mixed mustard and onion seeds

3 dried red chillies

4 curry leaves

2 tbsp lemon juice

1 To make the dosas, soak the rice and urid dhal for 3 hours. Grind the rice and urid dhal to a smooth consistency, adding water if necessary. Set aside for a further 3 hours to ferment. Alternatively, if you are using ground rice and urid dhal flour (ata), mix together in a bowl. Add the water and salt and stir until a batter is formed.

2 Heat about 1 tablespoon of oil in a large, non-stick, frying-pan. Using a ladle, spoon the batter into the frying-pan. Tilt the frying-pan to spread the mixture over the base. Cover and cook over a medium heat for about 2 minutes. Remove the lid and turn the dosa over very carefully. Pour a little oil around the edge, cover and cook for a further 2 minutes. Repeat with the remaining batter.

3 To make the filling, cook the potatoes in a pan of boiling water. Add the chillies, turmeric and salt and cook until the potatoes are just soft. Drain and mash lightly with a fork.

4 Heat the vegetable oil in a saucepan and fry the mustard and onion seeds, dried red chillies and curry leaves, stirring constantly, for about 1 minute. Pour the spice mixture over the mashed potatoes, then sprinkle over the lemon juice and mix well. Spoon the potato filling on one half of each of the dosas and fold the other half over it. Transfer to a warmed serving dish and serve hot.

Potato Curry

Served hot with pooris, this curry makes an excellent brunch with mango chutney as the perfect accompaniment.

NUTRITIONAL INFORMATION

Calories	390	Sugars	.......0.7g
Protein	.........2g	Fat	..........34g
Carbohydrate	...19g	Saturates	.......4g

 10 mins   25 mins

SERVES 4

I N G R E D I E N T S

3 medium potatoes

150 ml/5 fl oz vegetable oil

1 tsp onion seeds

½ tsp fennel seeds

4 curry leaves

1 tsp ground cumin

1 tsp ground coriander

1 tsp chilli powder

pinch of turmeric

1 tsp salt

1½ tsp dried mango powder

1 Peel and rinse the potatoes. Using a sharp knife, cut each potato into 6 slices.

2 Cook the potato slices in a saucepan of boiling water until just cooked, but not mushy (test by piercing with a sharp knife or a skewer). Drain and set aside until required.

3 Heat the vegetable oil in a separate, heavy-based saucepan over a moderate heat. Reduce the heat and add the onion seeds, fennel seeds and curry leaves and stir thoroughly.

4 Remove the pan from the heat and add the ground cumin, coriander, chilli powder, turmeric, salt and dried mango powder, stirring well to combine.

5 Return the pan to a low heat and fry the mixture, stirring constantly, for about 1 minute.

6 Pour this mixture over the cooked potatoes, mix together and stir-fry over a low heat for about 5 minutes.

7 Transfer the potato curry to serving dishes and serve immediately.

COOK'S TIP

Traditionally, semolina dessert is served to follow Potato Curry.

Indian Potatoes & Peas

This quick and easy-to-prepare Indian dish can be served either as an accompaniment or on its own with chapatis.

NUTRITIONAL INFORMATION

Calories	434	Sugars	.........6g
Protein	.........5g	Fat	..........35g
Carbohydrate	...28g	Saturates	.......4g

 15 mins 25 mins

SERVES 4

I N G R E D I E N T S

150 ml/5 fl oz vegetable oil

3 onions, sliced

1 tsp crushed garlic

1 tsp finely chopped fresh root ginger

1 tsp chilli powder

½ tsp turmeric

1 tsp salt

2 fresh green chillies, finely chopped

300 ml/10 fl oz water

675 g/1½ lb potatoes

100 g/3½ oz peas

TO GARNISH

chopped red chillies

fresh coriander leaves

1 Heat the oil in a large, heavy-based frying pan. Add the onions to the frying pan and fry, stirring occasionally, until the onions are golden brown.

2 Mix together the garlic, ginger, chilli powder, turmeric, salt and fresh green chillies. Add the spice mixture to the onions in the pan.

3 Stir in 150 ml/5 fl oz of the water, cover and cook until the onions are cooked through.

4 Meanwhile, cut the potatoes into six slices each, using a sharp knife.

5 Add the potato slices to the mixture in the pan and stir-fry for 5 minutes.

6 Add the peas and the remaining water to the pan, cover and cook for 7–10 minutes.

7 Transfer the potatoes and peas to serving plates and serve, garnished with chopped red chillies and coriander leaves.

COOK'S TIP

Turmeric is an aromatic root that is dried and ground to produce the distinctive bright yellow-orange powder used in many Indian dishes. It has a warm, aromatic smell and a full, somewhat musty taste.

Chickpea Curry

This curry is very popular in India. There are many different ways of cooking chickpeas, but this version is probably one of the most delicious.

NUTRITIONAL INFORMATION

Calories 114   Sugars 1.9g
Protein . . . . .2.9g   Fat 7.3g
Carbohydrate . .10.1g   Saturates 0.7g

5–10 mins   15 mins

SERVES 4

I N G R E D I E N T S

6 tbsp vegetable oil

2 onions, sliced

1 tsp finely chopped fresh root ginger

1 tsp ground cumin

1 tsp ground coriander

1 tsp fresh garlic, crushed

1 tsp chilli powder

2 fresh green chillies

1 tbsp fresh coriander leaves

150 ml/5 fl oz water

300 g/10½ oz potatoes

400 g/14 oz canned chickpeas, drained

1 tbsp lemon juice

1 Heat the oil in a large saucepan over a medium heat.

2 Add the onions to the pan and fry, stirring occasionally, until they are golden brown.

3 Reduce the heat, add the ginger, ground cumin, ground coriander, garlic, chilli powder, fresh green chillies and fresh coriander leaves to the pan and stir-fry for 2 minutes.

4 Add the water to the mixture in the pan and stir to mix.

5 Using a sharp knife, cut the potato into small cubes.

6 Add the potatoes and the drained chickpeas to the mixture in the pan, cover and leave to simmer, stirring occasionally, for 5–7 minutes.

7 Sprinkle the lemon juice over the curry.

8 Transfer the chickpea curry to serving dishes. Serve the curry hot with chapatis, if you wish.

COOK'S TIP

Using canned chickpeas saves time, but you can use dried chickpeas if you prefer. Soak them overnight, then boil them for 15–20 minutes or until soft.

Mixed Vegetables

This is a very popular vegetarian recipe. You can make it with any vegetables you choose, but the combination below is ideal.

NUTRITIONAL INFORMATION

Calories	669	Sugars	......17g
Protein	......7g	Fat	......57g
Carbohydrate	...36g	Saturates	.....8g

5 mins | 45 mins

SERVES 4

I N G R E D I E N T S

300 ml/10 fl oz vegetable oil

1 tsp mustard seeds

1 tsp onion seeds

½ tsp white cumin seeds

3–4 curry leaves, chopped

450 g/1 lb onions, finely chopped

3 tomatoes, chopped

½ red and ½ green pepper, sliced

1 tsp finely chopped fresh root ginger

1 tsp fresh garlic, crushed

1 tsp chilli powder

¼ tsp turmeric

1 tsp salt

425 ml/15 fl oz water

450 g/1 lb potatoes, cut into pieces

½ cauliflower, cut into small florets

4 carrots, peeled and sliced

3 green chillies, finely chopped

1 tbsp fresh coriander leaves

1 tbsp lemon juice

1 Heat the oil in a large saucepan. Add the mustard, onion and white cumin seeds along with the curry leaves and fry until they turn a shade darker.

2 Add the onions to the pan and fry over a medium heat until golden brown.

3 Add the tomatoes and peppers and stir-fry for approximately 5 minutes.

4 Add the ginger, garlic, chilli powder, turmeric and salt and mix well.

5 Add 300 ml/10 fl oz of the water, cover and leave to simmer for 10–12 minutes, stirring occasionally.

6 Add the potatoes, cauliflower, carrots, green chillies and coriander leaves and stir-fry for about 5 minutes.

7 Add the remaining water and the lemon juice, stirring to combine. Cover and leave to simmer for about 15 minutes, stirring occasionally.

8 Transfer the mixed vegetables to serving plates and serve immediately.

Pakoras

Pakoras are eaten all over India. They are made in many different ways and with a variety of fillings. Sometimes they are served with yogurt.

NUTRITIONAL INFORMATION

Calories 331	Sugars 5g
Protein 9g	Fat 22g
Carbohydrate . . .27g	Saturates 3g

 15 mins   15–20 mins

SERVES 4

I N G R E D I E N T S

6 tbsp gram flour

½ tsp salt

1 tsp chilli powder

1 tsp baking powder

1½ tsp white cumin seeds

1 tsp pomegranate seeds

300 ml/10 fl oz water

1 tbsp finely chopped fresh coriander

vegetables of your choice: cauliflower cut into small florets, onions cut into rings, sliced potatoes, sliced aubergines or fresh spinach leaves

vegetable oil, for deep-frying

1 Sift the gram flour into a large mixing bowl. Add the salt, chilli powder, baking powder, cumin and pomegranate seeds and blend together well. Pour in the water and beat thoroughly to form a smooth batter.

2 Add the coriander and mix. Set the batter aside.

3 Dip the prepared vegetables of your choice into the batter, carefully shaking off any of the excess batter.

4 Heat the oil in a large heavy-based pan. Place the battered vegetables of your choice in the oil and deep-fry, in batches, turning once.

5 Repeat this process until all of the batter has been used up.

6 Transfer the battered vegetables to kitchen paper and drain thoroughly. Serve immediately.

COOK'S TIP
When deep-frying, it is important to use oil at the correct temperature. If the oil is too hot, the outside of the food will burn as will the spices, before the inside is cooked. If the oil is too cool, the food will be sodden with oil before a crisp batter forms.

Potato & Lemon Casserole

This is based on a Moroccan dish in which potatoes are spiced with coriander and cumin and cooked in a lemon sauce.

NUTRITIONAL INFORMATION

Calories 338   Sugars 8g
Protein . . . . .5g   Fat 23g
Carbohydrate . . .29g   Saturates 2g

 15 mins   35 mins

SERVES 4

INGREDIENTS

100 ml/3½ fl oz olive oil

2 red onions, cut into eight

3 garlic cloves, crushed

2 tsp ground cumin

2 tsp ground coriander

pinch of cayenne pepper

1 carrot, thickly sliced

2 small turnips, quartered

1 courgette, sliced

500 g/1 lb 2 oz potatoes, thickly sliced

juice and rind of 2 large lemons

300 ml/10 fl oz vegetable stock

2 tbsp chopped fresh coriander

salt and pepper

COOK'S TIP

Check the vegetables while they are cooking, because they may begin to stick to the pan. Add a little more boiling water or stock if necessary.

1 Heat the olive oil in a flameproof casserole. Add the onion and sauté over a medium heat, stirring frequently, for 3 minutes.

2 Add the garlic and cook for 30 seconds. Stir in the spices and cook, stirring constantly, for 1 minute.

3 Add the carrot, turnips, courgette and potatoes and stir to coat in the oil.

4 Add the lemon juice and rind and the vegetable stock. Season to taste with salt and pepper. Cover and cook over a medium heat, stirring occasionally, for 20–30 minutes, until tender.

5 Remove the lid, sprinkle in the coriander and stir well. Serve immediately.

Tofu & Vegetable Stir-fry

This is a quick dish to prepare, making it ideal as a midweek supper dish, after a busy day at work!

NUTRITIONAL INFORMATION

Calories 124   Sugars 2g
Protein ....6g   Fat 6g
Carbohydrate ....11g   Saturates 1g

 5 mins   25 mins

SERVES 4

INGREDIENTS

175 g/6 oz potatoes, cubed

1 tbsp vegetable oil

1 red onion, sliced

225 g/8 oz firm tofu, diced

2 courgettes, diced

8 canned artichoke hearts, halved

150 ml/5 fl oz passata

1 tbsp sweet chilli sauce

1 tbsp soy sauce

1 tsp caster sugar

2 tbsp chopped fresh basil

salt and pepper

1 Cook the potatoes in a saucepan of boiling water for 10 minutes. Drain thoroughly and set aside until required.

2 Heat the vegetable oil in a wok or large frying pan and sauté the red onion for 2 minutes until the onion has softened, stirring.

3 Stir in the tofu and courgettes and cook for 3–4 minutes until they begin to brown slightly.

4 Add the cooked potatoes to the wok or frying pan, stirring to mix.

5 Stir in the artichoke hearts, passata, sweet chilli sauce, soy sauce, sugar and basil.

6 Season to taste with salt and pepper and cook for a further 5 minutes, stirring well.

7 Transfer the tofu and vegetable stir-fry to serving dishes and serve immediately.

COOK'S TIP

Canned artichoke hearts should be drained thoroughly and rinsed before use because they often have salt added.

Jacket Potatoes with Beans

Baked jacket potatoes, topped with a tasty mixture of beans in a spicy sauce, provide a deliciously filling, high-fibre dish.

NUTRITIONAL INFORMATION

Calories ....378 Sugars 9g
Protein ....15g Fat 9g
Carbohydrate ...64g Saturates 1g

  15 mins 1 hr 15 mins

SERVES 6

INGREDIENTS

1.8 kg/4 lb potatoes

4 tbsp vegetable ghee or oil

1 large onion, chopped

2 garlic cloves, crushed

1 tsp ground turmeric

1 tbsp cumin seeds

2 tbsp mild or medium curry paste

350 g/12 oz cherry tomatoes

400 g/14 oz canned black-eyed beans,
    drained and rinsed

400 g/14 oz canned red kidney beans,
    drained and rinsed

1 tbsp lemon juice

2 tbsp tomato purée

150 ml/5 fl oz water

2 tbsp chopped fresh mint or coriander

salt and pepper

VARIATION

Instead of cutting the potatoes in half, cut a cross in each and squeeze gently to open out. Spoon some of the prepared filling into the cross and place any remaining filling to the side.

1 Scrub the potatoes and prick several times with a fork. Place in a preheated oven, 180°C/350°F/Gas Mark 4, and cook for 1–1¼ hours, or until the potatoes feel soft when gently squeezed.

2 About 20 minutes before the end of cooking time, prepare the topping. Heat the ghee or oil in a saucepan, add the onion and cook over a low heat, stirring frequently, for 5 minutes. Add the garlic, turmeric, cumin seeds and curry paste and cook gently for 1 minute.

3 Stir in the tomatoes, black-eyed beans and red kidney beans, lemon juice, tomato purée, water and mint or coriander. Season to taste with salt and pepper, then cover and simmer over a low heat, stirring frequently, for 10 minutes.

4 When the potatoes are cooked, cut them in half and mash the flesh lightly with a fork. Spoon the prepared bean mixture on top, place on warming serving plates and serve immediately.

Yellow Curry

Potatoes are not highly regarded in Thai cookery, because rice is the traditional staple. This dish is a tasty exception.

NUTRITIONAL INFORMATION

Calories 160
Sugars 4g
Protein 3g
Fat 10g
Carbohydrate . . .15g
Saturates 1g

 5 mins   15 mins

SERVES 4

I N G R E D I E N T S

2 garlic cloves, finely chopped

3-cm/1¼-inch piece galangal, finely chopped

1 lemon grass, finely chopped

1 tsp coriander seeds

3 tbsp vegetable oil

2 tsp Thai red curry paste

½ tsp turmeric

200 ml/7 fl oz coconut milk

250 g/9 oz potatoes, cubed

100 ml/3½ fl oz vegetable stock

200 g/7 oz young spinach leaves

1 small onion, thinly sliced into rings

1 Place the garlic, galangal, lemon grass and coriander seeds in a pestle and mortar and pound continuously until a smooth paste forms.

2 Heat 2 tablespoons of the oil in a frying pan or wok. Stir in the garlic paste and stir-fry for 30 seconds. Stir in the curry paste and turmeric, then add the coconut milk and bring the mixture to the boil.

3 Add the potatoes and stock. Return to the boil, then lower the heat and simmer, uncovered, for 10–12 minutes until the potatoes are almost tender.

4 Stir in the spinach and simmer until the leaves are wilted.

5 Fry the onion in the remaining oil until crisp and golden brown. Place on top of the curry just before serving.

COOK'S TIP
Choose a firm, waxy potato for this dish, one that will keep its shape during cooking, in preference to a floury variety that will break up easily once cooked.

Sweet Potato Cakes

Enticing little tasty mouthfuls of sweet potato, served hot and sizzling from the pan with a delicious fresh tomato sauce.

NUTRITIONAL INFORMATION

Calories 349	Sugars 9g	
Protein 4g	Fat 24g	
Carbohydrate . . .32g	Saturates 3g	

  10–15 mins   15 mins

SERVES 4

I N G R E D I E N T S

500 g/1 lb 2 oz sweet potatoes

2 garlic cloves, crushed

1 small green chilli, chopped

2 sprigs coriander, chopped

1 tbsp dark soy sauce

plain flour, for shaping

vegetable oil, for frying

sesame seeds, for sprinkling

S O Y - T O M A T O   S A U C E

2 tsp vegetable oil

1 garlic clove, finely chopped

1½ tsp finely chopped fresh root ginger

3 tomatoes, skinned and chopped

2 tbsp dark soy sauce

1 tbsp lime juice

2 tbsp chopped fresh coriander

1 To make the soy-tomato sauce, heat the oil in a wok and stir-fry the garlic and ginger for about 1 minute. Add the tomatoes and stir-fry for a further 2 minutes. Remove from the heat and stir in the soy sauce, lime juice and coriander. Set aside and keep warm.

2 Peel the sweet potatoes and grate finely (you can do this quickly with a food processor). Place the garlic, chilli and coriander in a pestle and mortar and crush to a smooth paste. Stir in the soy sauce and mix with the sweet potatoes.

3 Divide the mixture into 12 equal portions. Dip into flour and pat into a flat, round patty shape.

4 Heat a shallow layer of oil in a wide frying pan. Fry the sweet potato patties in batches over a high heat until golden, turning once.

5 Drain on kitchen paper and sprinkle with sesame seeds. Serve hot, with a spoonful of the soy-tomato sauce.

COOK'S TIP

Make sure that the potatoes are sliced very thinly so that they are almost transparent. This will ensure that they cook thoroughly.

Vegetable Savouries

This chapter proves that meat does not have to be involved in a truly excellent main meal. In this section you will find dishes from all over the world, such as Potato & Spinach Gnocchi from Italy, and Vegetable Pulao from India. Family favourites such as

Nutty Harvest Loaf and Vegetable Hotpot have been included, while the needs of the dinner party have not been forgotten with the spectacular Potato & Three Cheese Soufflé. Whatever the occasion, you are sure to find something to satisfy the heartiest of appetites.

Sweet Potato & Leek Patties

Sweet potatoes have very dense flesh and a delicious, sweet, earthy taste, which contrasts well with the pungent flavour of the ginger.

NUTRITIONAL INFORMATION

Calories 403	Sugars 34g
Protein 8g	Fat 12g
Carbohydrate . . .67g	Saturates 2g

15 mins,
plus 30 mins
chilling time

40 mins

SERVES 4

INGREDIENTS

900 g/2 lb sweet potatoes

4 tsp sunflower oil

2 leeks, trimmed and finely chopped

1 garlic clove, crushed

2 tsp finely chopped fresh root ginger

200 g/7 oz canned sweetcorn, drained

2 tbsp low-fat natural fromage frais

6 tbsp wholemeal flour

salt and pepper

GINGER SAUCE

2 tbsp white wine vinegar

2 tsp caster sugar

1 red chilli, seeded and chopped

2.5-cm/1-inch piece fresh root ginger, cut
  into thin strips

2 tbsp ginger wine

4 tbsp vegetable stock

1 tsp cornflour

TO SERVE

lettuce leaves

spring onions, shredded

1 Peel the potatoes, cut into thick cubes and boil for 10–15 minutes. Drain well and mash. Leave to cool.

2 Heat 2 teaspoons of the oil and fry the leeks, garlic and ginger for 2–3 minutes. Stir into the potato with the sweetcorn, seasoning and fromage frais. Form into 8 patties and toss in the flour. Chill for 30 minutes. Place the patties on a preheated grill rack and lightly brush with oil. Grill for 5 minutes, then turn over, brush with oil and grill for a further 5 minutes.

3 To make the sauce, place the vinegar, sugar, chilli and ginger in a pan and simmer for 5 minutes. Stir in the wine. Blend the stock and cornflour and add to the sauce, stirring, until thickened. Serve the patties with lettuce and spring onions, and the sauce.

  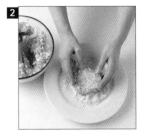

Ratatouille Vegetable Grill

Ratatouille is a classic dish of vegetables cooked in a tomato and herb sauce. Here it is topped with diced potatoes and cheese.

NUTRITIONAL INFORMATION

Calories . . . . . . .287 Sugars 13g
Protein . . . . .14g Fat 4g
Carbohydrate . . .53g Saturates 2g

15 mins   25 mins

SERVES 4

INGREDIENTS

2 onions

1 garlic clove

1 red pepper

1 green pepper

1 aubergine

2 courgettes

800 g/1 lb 12 oz canned chopped tomatoes

1 bouquet garni

2 tbsp tomato purée

900 g/2 lb potatoes

75 g/2¾ oz reduced-fat mature Cheddar cheese, grated

salt and pepper

2 tbsp snipped fresh chives, to garnish

1 Peel and finely chop the onions and garlic. Rinse, deseed and slice the peppers. Rinse, trim and cut the aubergine into small cubes. Rinse, trim and thinly slice the courgettes.

2 Place the onion, garlic and peppers into a large saucepan. Add the tomatoes, and stir in the bouquet garni, tomato purée and salt and pepper to taste. Bring to the boil, cover and simmer for 10 minutes, stirring half-way through. Stir in the prepared aubergine and courgettes and cook, uncovered, for a further 10 minutes, stirring occasionally.

3 Meanwhile, peel the potatoes and cut into 2.5-cm/ 1-inch cubes. Place the potatoes into another saucepan and cover with water. Bring to the boil and cook for 10–12 minutes until tender. Drain and set aside.

4 Transfer the vegetables on to a heatproof gratin dish. Arrange the cooked potatoes evenly over the vegetables.

5 Preheat the grill to medium. Sprinkle grated cheese over the potatoes and place under the grill for 5 minutes until golden, bubbling and hot. Serve garnished with snipped chives.

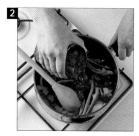

VARIATION

You can vary the vegetables in this dish depending on seasonal availability and personal preference. Try broccoli, carrots or sweetcorn, if you prefer.

Potato & Pepperoni Pizza

Potatoes make a great pizza base and this recipe is well worth making, rather than using a ready-made base, both for texture and flavour.

NUTRITIONAL INFORMATION

Calories 234   Sugars 5g
Protein ....4g   Fat 12g
Carbohydrate ...30g   Saturates 1g

20 mins   45 mins

SERVES 4

I N G R E D I E N T S

900 g/2 lb floury potatoes, diced

1 tbsp butter

2 garlic cloves, crushed

2 tbsp mixed chopped fresh herbs

1 egg, beaten

6 tbsp passata

2 tbsp tomato purée

50 g/1¾ oz pepperoni slices

1 green pepper, cut into strips

1 yellow pepper, cut into strips

2 large open-cap mushrooms, sliced

25 g/1 oz stoned black olives, quartered

125 g/4½ oz mozzarella cheese, sliced

1 Grease and flour a 23-cm/9-inch pizza tin.

2 Cook the diced potatoes in a saucepan of boiling water for 10 minutes or until cooked through. Drain and mash until smooth. Transfer the mashed potato to a mixing bowl and stir in the butter, garlic, herbs and egg.

3 Spread the mixture into the prepared pizza tin. Cook in a preheated oven, at 220°C/425°F/Gas Mark 7, for 7–10 minutes or until the pizza base begins to set.

4 Mix the passata and tomato purée together and spoon it over the pizza base, to within 1 cm/½ inch of the edge of the base.

5 Arrange the pepperoni slices and the peppers, mushrooms and olives on top of the passata.

6 Scatter the mozzarella cheese on top of the pizza. Return to the oven for 20 minutes or until the base is cooked through and the cheese has melted on top. Serve hot.

COOK'S TIP

This pizza base is softer in texture than a normal bread dough and is ideal served from the tin. Top with any of your favourite pizza ingredients that you have to hand.

Potato & Spinach Gnocchi

These small potato dumplings are flavoured with spinach, cooked in boiling water and served with a simple tomato sauce.

NUTRITIONAL INFORMATION

Calories 315   Sugars 7g
Protein . . . . .8g   Fat 8g
Carbohydrate . . .56g   Saturates 1g

 20 mins   30 mins

SERVES 4

INGREDIENTS

300 g/10½ oz floury potatoes, diced

175 g/6 oz spinach

1 egg yolk

1 tsp olive oil

125 g/4½ oz plain flour

salt and pepper

spinach leaves, to garnish

SAUCE

1 tbsp olive oil

2 shallots, chopped

1 garlic clove, crushed

300 ml/10 fl oz passata

2 tsp soft light brown sugar

1 Cook the diced potatoes in a saucepan of boiling water for 10 minutes or until cooked through. Drain thoroughly, then mash the potatoes.

2 Meanwhile, in a separate pan, blanch the spinach in a little boiling water for 1–2 minutes. Drain the spinach and shred the leaves.

3 Transfer the mashed potato to a lightly floured chopping board and make a well in the centre. Add the egg yolk, olive oil, spinach, salt and pepper and a little of the flour and quickly mix the ingredients into the potato, adding more flour as you go, until you have a firm dough. Divide the mixture into very small dumplings.

4 Cook the gnocchi, in batches, in a saucepan of boiling salted water for approximately 5 minutes or until they rise to the surface.

5 Meanwhile, to make the sauce, put the oil, shallots, garlic, passata and sugar into a saucepan and cook over a low heat for 10–15 minutes or until the sauce has thickened.

6 Drain the gnocchi using a perforated spoon and transfer to warm serving dishes. Spoon the sauce over the gnocchi and garnish with the fresh spinach leaves.

VARIATION

Add chopped fresh herbs and cheese to the gnocchi dough instead of the spinach, if you prefer.

Potato-topped Vegetables

This is a very colourful and nutritious dish, packed full of crunchy vegetables in a tasty white wine sauce.

NUTRITIONAL INFORMATION

Calories 413   Sugars 11g
Protein . . . . .19g   Fat 18g
Carbohydrate . . .41g   Saturates 11g

20 mins   1 hr 15 mins

SERVES 4

INGREDIENTS

1 carrot, diced

175 g/6 oz cauliflower florets

175 g/6 oz broccoli florets

1 fennel bulb, sliced

75 g/2¾ oz green beans, halved

2 tbsp butter

2½ tbsp plain flour

150 ml/5 fl oz vegetable stock

150 ml/5 fl oz dry white wine

150 ml/5 fl oz milk

175 g/6 oz chestnut mushrooms, quartered

2 tbsp chopped fresh sage

TOPPING

900 g/2 lb floury potatoes, diced

2 tbsp butter

4 tbsp natural yogurt

70 g/2½ oz Parmesan cheese, freshly grated

1 tsp fennel seeds

salt and pepper

1 Cook the carrot, cauliflower, broccoli, fennel and beans in a large saucepan of boiling water for 10 minutes, until just tender. Drain the vegetables thoroughly and set aside.

2 Melt the butter in a saucepan. Stir in the flour and cook for 1 minute. Remove from the heat and stir in the stock, wine and milk. Return to the heat and bring to the boil, stirring until thickened. Stir in the reserved vegetables, mushrooms and sage.

3 Meanwhile, make the topping. Cook the potatoes in boiling water for

10–15 minutes. Drain and mash with the butter, yogurt and half the cheese. Stir in the fennel seeds. Season to taste.

4 Spoon the vegetable mixture into a 1-litre/1¾-pint pie dish. Spoon the potato over the top and sprinkle with the remaining cheese. Cook in a preheated oven, 190°C/375°F/Gas Mark 5, for 30–35 minutes, or until golden. Serve hot.

Three Cheese Soufflé

This soufflé is very simple to make, yet it has a delicious flavour and melts in the mouth. Choose three alternative cheeses, if preferred.

NUTRITIONAL INFORMATION

Calories 447   Sugars 1g
Protein . . . . .22g   Fat 23g
Carbohydrate . . .41g   Saturates 11g

 10 mins   55 mins

SERVES 4

INGREDIENTS

2 tbsp butter

2 tsp plain flour

900 g/2 lb floury potatoes

8 eggs, separated

25 g/1 oz Gruyère cheese, grated

25 g/1 oz blue cheese, crumbled

25 g/1 oz mature Cheddar cheese, grated

salt and pepper

3 Beat the egg yolks into the potato and stir in the Gruyère cheese, blue cheese and Cheddar, mixing well. Season to taste with salt and pepper.

4 Whisk the egg whites until standing in peaks, then gently fold them into the potato mixture with a metal spoon until fully incorporated.

5 Spoon the potato mixture into the prepared soufflé dish.

6 Cook in a preheated oven, 220°C/ 425°F/Gas Mark 7, for 35–40 minutes, until risen and set. Serve immediately.

1 Butter a 2.2-litre/4-pint soufflé dish and dust with the flour. Set aside.

2 Cook the potatoes in a saucepan of boiling water until tender. Mash until very smooth and then transfer to a mixing bowl to cool.

COOK'S TIP

Insert a fine skewer into the centre of the soufflé; it should come out clean when the soufflé is fully cooked through.

Nutty Harvest Loaf

This attractive and nutritious loaf is also utterly delicious. Served with a fresh tomato sauce, it can be eaten hot or cold with salad.

NUTRITIONAL INFORMATION

Calories ....554 Sugars 12g
Protein ....16g Fat 37g
Carbohydrate ...43g Saturates 16g

 20 mins   1 hr 20 mins

SERVES 4

INGREDIENTS

2 tbsp butter, plus extra
   for greasing

450 g/1 lb floury potatoes, diced

1 onion, chopped

2 garlic cloves, crushed

125 g/4½ oz unsalted peanuts

75 g/2¾ oz fresh white breadcrumbs

1 egg, beaten

2 tbsp chopped fresh coriander

150 ml/5 fl oz vegetable stock

75 g/2¾ oz sliced mushrooms

50 g/1¾ oz sun-dried tomatoes, sliced

salt and pepper

SAUCE

150 ml/5 fl oz crème fraîche

2 tsp tomato purée

2 tsp clear honey

2 tbsp chopped fresh coriander

1 Grease a 450-g/1-lb loaf tin. Cook the potatoes in a saucepan of boiling water for 10 minutes, until cooked through. Drain well, mash and set aside.

2 Melt half of the butter in a frying pan. Add the onion and garlic and fry gently for 2–3 minutes, until soft. Finely chop the nuts or process them in a food processor for 30 seconds with the breadcrumbs.

3 Mix the chopped nuts and breadcrumbs into the potatoes with the egg, coriander and vegetable stock. Stir in the onion and garlic and mix well.

4 Melt the remaining butter in the frying pan, add the sliced mushrooms and cook for 2–3 minutes.

5 Press half of the potato mixture into the base of the loaf tin. Spoon the mushrooms on top and sprinkle with the sun-dried tomatoes. Spoon the remaining potato mixture on top and smooth the surface. Cover with foil and bake in a preheated oven, 190°C/375°F/Gas Mark 5, for 1 hour, or until firm to the touch.

6 Meanwhile, mix the sauce ingredients together. Cut the nutty harvest loaf into slices and serve with the sauce.

Vegetable Cake

This is a savoury version of a cheesecake with a layer of fried potatoes as a delicious base. Use frozen mixed vegetables for the topping, if you like.

NUTRITIONAL INFORMATION

Calories 502   Sugars 8g
Protein ....16g   Fat 31g
Carbohydrate ...41g   Saturates 14g

 20 mins   45 mins

SERVES 4

INGREDIENTS

BASE

2 tbsp vegetable oil, plus extra for brushing

1.25 kg/2 lb 12 oz waxy potatoes, thinly sliced

TOPPING

1 tbsp vegetable oil

1 leek, chopped

1 courgette, grated

1 red pepper, deseeded and diced

1 green pepper, deseeded and diced

1 carrot, grated

2 tsp chopped parsley

225 g/8 oz full-fat soft cheese

25 g/1 oz mature cheese, grated

2 eggs, beaten

salt and pepper

shredded cooked leek, to garnish

salad, to serve

1 Brush a 20-cm/8-inch springform cake tin with oil.

2 To make the base, heat the oil in a frying pan. Cook the potato slices until softened and browned. Drain on kitchen paper and place in the base of the tin.

3 To make the topping, heat the oil in a separate frying pan. Add the leek and fry over a low heat, stirring frequently, for 3–4 minutes, until softened.

4 Add the courgette, peppers, carrot and parsley to the pan and cook over a low heat for 5–7 minutes, or until the vegetables have softened.

5 Meanwhile, beat the cheeses and eggs together in a bowl. Stir in the vegetables and season to taste with salt and pepper. Spoon the mixture evenly over the potato base.

6 Cook in a preheated oven, 190°C/ 375°F/Gas Mark 5, for 20–25 minutes, until the cake is set.

7 Remove the vegetable cake from the tin, transfer to a warm serving plate, garnish with shredded leek and serve with a crisp salad.

Potato Hash

This is a variation of the American dish, beef hash, which was made with salt beef and leftovers, and served to seafaring New Englanders.

NUTRITIONAL INFORMATION

Calories ....302 Sugars 5g
Protein ....15g Fat 10g
Carbohydrate ...40g Saturates 4g

10 mins   30 mins

SERVES 4

INGREDIENTS

2 tbsp butter

1 red onion, halved and sliced

1 carrot, diced

25 g/1 oz green beans, halved

900 g/2 lb waxy potatoes, diced

2 tbsp plain flour

600 ml/1 pint vegetable stock

225 g/8 oz tofu, diced

salt and pepper

chopped fresh parsley, to garnish

1 Melt the butter in a large, heavy-based frying pan. Add the onion, carrot, green beans and potatoes and fry over a fairly low heat, stirring constantly, for about 5–7 minutes, or until the vegetables begin to turn golden brown.

2 Add the flour to the frying pan and cook, stirring constantly, for 1 minute. Gradually pour in the stock, stirring constantly.

3 Reduce the heat to low and simmer for 15 minutes, or until the potatoes are tender.

4 Add the diced tofu to the pan and cook for a further 5 minutes. Season to taste with salt and pepper.

5 Sprinkle the chopped fresh parsley over the top of the potato hash to garnish and then serve it hot straight from the frying pan.

COOK'S TIP

Hash is an American term meaning to chop food into small pieces. Therefore a traditional hash dish is made from chopped fresh ingredients, such as peppers, onion and celery.

Twice Baked Pesto Potatoes

This is an easy, but very filling meal. The potatoes are baked until fluffy, then they are mixed with a tasty pesto filling and baked again.

NUTRITIONAL INFORMATION

Calories . . . . . . .444 Sugars 3g
Protein . . . . .10g Fat 28g
Carbohydrate . . .40g Saturates 13g

 10 mins 1 hr 20 mins

SERVES 4

INGREDIENTS

4 baking potatoes

150 ml/5 fl oz double cream

5 tbsp vegetable stock

1 tbsp lemon juice

2 garlic cloves, crushed

3 tbsp chopped fresh basil

2 tbsp pine kernels

35 g/1¼ oz Parmesan cheese, freshly grated

salt and pepper

1 Scrub the potatoes well and prick the skins with a fork. Rub a little salt into the skins and place on a baking tray.

2 Cook in a preheated oven, 190°C/ 375°F/Gas Mark 5, for 1 hour, or until the potatoes are cooked through and the skins are crisp.

3 Remove the potatoes from the oven and cut them in half lengthways. Using a spoon, scoop the potato flesh into a mixing bowl, leaving a thin shell of potato inside the skins. Mash the potato flesh with a fork.

4 Meanwhile, mix the cream and stock in a saucepan and simmer over a low heat for about 8–10 minutes, or until reduced by half.

5 Stir in the lemon juice, garlic and chopped basil and season to taste with salt and pepper. Stir the mixture into the mashed potato flesh, together with the pine kernels.

6 Spoon the mixture back into the potato shells and sprinkle the Parmesan cheese on top. Return the potatoes to the oven for 10 minutes, or until the cheese has browned. Serve hot.

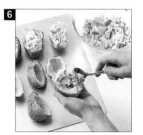

VARIATION

Add full-fat soft cheese or thinly sliced mushrooms to the mashed potato flesh in step 5, if you prefer.

Potato & Aubergine Gratin

Similar to a simple moussaka, this recipe is made up of layers of aubergine, tomato and potato baked with a yogurt topping.

NUTRITIONAL INFORMATION

Calories	409	Sugars	........17g
Protein	........28g	Fat	..........14g
Carbohydrate	...45g	Saturates	.......3g

  25 mins   1 hr 15 mins

SERVES 4

INGREDIENTS

500 g/1 lb 2 oz waxy potatoes, sliced

1 tbsp vegetable oil

1 onion, chopped

2 garlic cloves, crushed

500 g/1 lb 2 oz tofu, diced

2 tbsp tomato purée

2 tbsp plain flour

300 ml/10 fl oz vegetable stock

2 large tomatoes, sliced

1 aubergine, sliced

2 tbsp chopped fresh thyme

450 ml/16 fl oz natural yogurt

2 eggs, beaten

salt and pepper

salad, to serve

VARIATION

You can use marinated or smoked tofu for extra flavour, if you wish.

1 Cook the sliced potatoes in a saucepan of boiling water for 10 minutes, until tender, but not breaking up. Drain and set aside.

2 Heat the oil in a frying pan. Add the onion and garlic and fry, stirring occasionally, for 2–3 minutes.

3 Add the tofu, tomato purée and flour and cook for 1 minute. Gradually stir in the stock and bring to the boil, stirring. Reduce the heat and simmer for 10 minutes.

4 Arrange a layer of the potato slices in the base of a deep ovenproof dish.

Spoon the tofu mixture evenly on top. Layer the sliced tomatoes, then the aubergine and finally, the remaining potato slices on top of the tofu mixture, making sure that it is completely covered. Sprinkle with thyme.

5 Mix the yogurt and beaten eggs together in a bowl and season to taste with salt and pepper. Spoon the yogurt topping over the sliced potatoes to cover them completely.

6 Bake in a preheated oven, 190°C/ 375°F/Gas Mark 5, for about 35–45 minutes or until the topping is browned. Serve with a crisp salad.

Spicy Potato & Nut Terrine

This delicious baked terrine has a base of mashed potato flavoured with nuts, cheese, herbs and spices.

NUTRITIONAL INFORMATION

Calories 1100   Sugars 13g
Protein . . . . .34g   Fat 93g
Carbohydrate . . .31g   Saturates 22g

 15 mins   1 hr 20 mins

SERVES 4

INGREDIENTS

225 g/8 oz floury potatoes, diced

225 g/8 oz pecan nuts

225 g/8 oz unsalted cashew nuts

1 onion, finely chopped

2 garlic cloves, crushed

125 g/4½ oz open-cap mushrooms, diced

2 tbsp butter

2 tbsp chopped mixed herbs

1 tsp paprika

1 tsp ground cumin

1 tsp ground coriander

4 eggs, beaten

125 g/4½ oz full-fat soft cheese

60 g/2 oz Parmesan cheese, freshly grated

salt and pepper

SAUCE

3 large tomatoes, peeled, deseeded and chopped

2 tbsp tomato purée

5 tbsp red wine

1 tbsp red wine vinegar

pinch of caster sugar

1 Lightly grease a 900-g/2-lb loaf tin and line with baking paper.

2 Cook the potatoes in a large pan of lightly salted boiling water for 10 minutes, or until cooked through. Drain and mash thoroughly.

3 Finely chop the pecan and cashew nuts or process in a food processor. Mix the nuts with the onion, garlic and mushrooms. Melt the butter in a frying pan and cook the nut mixture for 5–7 minutes. Add the herbs and spices. Stir in the eggs, cheeses and potatoes and season to taste with salt and pepper.

4 Spoon the mixture into the prepared loaf tin, pressing it down quite firmly. Cook in a preheated oven, 190°C/375°F/Gas Mark 5, for 1 hour, or until set.

5 To make the sauce, mix the tomatoes, tomato purée, wine, wine vinegar and sugar in a pan and bring to the boil, stirring. Cook for 10 minutes, or until the tomatoes have reduced. Press the sauce through a sieve or process in a food processor for 30 seconds. Turn the terrine out of the tin on to a serving plate and cut into slices. Serve with the tomato sauce.

Potato & Tomato Calzone

These pizza dough Italian pasties are best served hot with a salad for a delicious lunch or supper dish.

NUTRITIONAL INFORMATION

Calories . . . . . . .524 Sugars 8g
Protein . . . . .17g Fat 8g
Carbohydrate . .103g Saturates 2g

20 mins, plus 1 hr rising time

35 mins

SERVES 4

INGREDIENTS

DOUGH

450 g/1 lb white bread flour

1 tsp easy-blend dried yeast

300 ml/10 fl oz vegetable stock

1 tbsp clear honey

1 tsp caraway seeds

skimmed milk, for glazing

FILLING

1 tbsp vegetable oil

225 g/8 oz waxy potatoes, diced

1 onion, halved and sliced

2 garlic cloves, crushed

40 g/1½ oz sun-dried tomatoes

2 tbsp chopped fresh basil

2 tbsp tomato purée

2 celery sticks, sliced

50 g/1¾ oz mozzarella cheese, grated

1 To make the dough, sift the flour into a large mixing bowl and stir in the yeast. Make a well in the centre of the mixture. Stir in the vegetable stock, honey and caraway seeds and bring the mixture together to form a dough.

2 Turn the dough out on to a lightly floured surface and knead for 8 minutes until smooth. Place the dough in a lightly oiled mixing bowl, cover and leave to rise in a warm place for 1 hour or until it has doubled in size.

3 Meanwhile, make the filling. Heat the oil in a frying pan and add all the remaining ingredients except for the cheese. Cook for about 5 minutes, stirring.

4 Divide the risen dough into 4 pieces. On a lightly floured surface, roll them out to form four 18-cm/ 7-inch circles. Spoon equal amounts of the filling on to one half of each circle. Sprinkle the cheese over the filling. Brush the edge of the dough with milk and fold the dough over to form 4 semi-circles, pressing to seal the edges.

5 Place on a non-stick baking tray and brush with milk. Cook in a preheated oven, 220°C/425°F/Gas Mark 7, for 30 minutes until golden and risen.

Potato-topped Lentil Bake

A wonderful mixture of red lentils, tofu and vegetables is cooked beneath a crunchy potato topping for a really hearty meal.

NUTRITIONAL INFORMATION

Calories	627	Sugars	.........7g
Protein	........26g	Fat	..........30g
Carbohydrate	...66g	Saturates	......13g

 10 mins   1 hr 30 mins

SERVES 4

INGREDIENTS

TOPPING

675 g/1½ lb floury potatoes, diced

2 tbsp butter

1 tbsp milk

50 g/1¾ oz pecan nuts, chopped

2 tbsp chopped fresh thyme

thyme sprigs, to garnish

FILLING

225 g/8 oz red lentils

5 tbsp butter

1 leek, sliced

2 garlic cloves, crushed

1 celery stick, chopped

125 g/4½ oz broccoli florets

175 g/6 oz smoked tofu, cubed

2 tsp tomato purée

salt and pepper

1 To make the topping, cook the potatoes in a saucepan of boiling water for 10–15 minutes, or until cooked through. Drain well, add the butter and milk and mash thoroughly. Stir in the pecan nuts and chopped thyme and set aside.

2 Cook the lentils in boiling water for 20–30 minutes, or until tender. Drain and set aside.

3 Melt the butter in a frying pan. Add the leek, garlic, celery and broccoli. Fry over a medium heat, stirring frequently, for 5 minutes, until softened.

Add the tofu cubes. Stir in the lentils, together with the tomato purée. Season with salt and pepper to taste, then turn the mixture into the base of a shallow ovenproof dish.

4 Spoon the mashed potato on top of the lentil mixture, spreading to cover it completely.

5 Cook in a preheated oven, 200°C/400°F/Gas Mark 6, for about 30–35 minutes, or until the topping is golden. Garnish with sprigs of fresh thyme and serve hot.

VARIATION

You can use almost any combination of your favourite vegetables in this dish.

Vegetable Pulao

This is a lovely way of cooking rice and vegetables together, and the saffron gives it a beautiful aroma. Serve this with any kebab.

NUTRITIONAL INFORMATION

Calories	557	Sugars	.........9g
Protein	........11g	Fat	..........14g
Carbohydrate	..104g	Saturates	.......7g

20 mins   55 mins

SERVES 6

INGREDIENTS

450 g/1 lb potatoes, cut into 12 pieces

1 aubergine, cut into 6 pieces

2 carrots, sliced

50 g/1¾ oz green beans, chopped

4 tbsp vegetable ghee

2 onions, sliced

175 ml/6 fl oz natural yogurt

2 tsp finely chopped fresh root ginger

2 tsp crushed garlic

2 tsp garam masala

2 tsp black cumin seeds

½ tsp turmeric

3 black cardamoms

3 cinnamon sticks

2 tsp salt

1 tsp chilli powder

½ tsp saffron strands

300 ml/10 fl oz milk

600 g/1 lb 5 oz basmati rice

5 tbsp lemon juice

TO GARNISH

4 green chillies, chopped

coriander leaves, chopped

1 Have the prepared vegetables to hand. Heat the ghee in a pan. Add the potatoes, aubergine, carrots and beans and fry, turning frequently, until softened. Remove from the pan and set aside.

2 Add the onions and fry, stirring frequently, until soft. Add the yogurt, ginger, garlic, garam masala, 1 teaspoon black cumin seeds, the turmeric, 1 cardamom, 1 cinnamon stick, 1 teaspoon salt and the chilli powder and stir-fry for 3–5 minutes. Return the vegetables to the pan and fry for 4–5 minutes.

3 Put the saffron and milk in a saucepan and bring to the boil, stirring. Remove from the heat and set aside.

4 In a pan of boiling water, half-cook the rice with 1 teaspoon salt, 2 cinnamon sticks, 2 black cardamoms and 1 teaspoon black cumin seeds. Drain the rice, leaving half in the pan, while transferring the other half to a bowl. Pour the vegetable mixture on top of the rice in the pan. Pour half of the lemon juice and half of the saffron milk over the vegetables and rice, cover with the remaining rice and pour the remaining lemon juice and saffron milk over the top. Garnish with chillies and coriander, return to the heat and cover. Cook over a low heat for about 20 minutes. Serve while hot.

Vegetable & Tofu Strudels

These strudels look really impressive and are perfect if friends are coming round or for a more formal dinner party dish.

NUTRITIONAL INFORMATION

Calories 485   Sugars 5g
Protein . . . . .16g   Fat 27g
Carbohydrate . . .47g   Saturates 5g

 25 mins   30 mins

SERVES 4

INGREDIENTS

FILLING

2 tbsp vegetable oil

2 tbsp butter

150 g/5½ oz potatoes, finely diced

1 leek, shredded

2 garlic cloves, crushed

1 tsp garam masala

½ tsp chilli powder

½ tsp turmeric

50 g/1¾ oz okra, sliced

100 g/3½ oz button mushrooms, sliced

2 tomatoes, diced

225 g/8 oz firm tofu, diced

salt and pepper

PASTRY CASES

350 g/12 oz (12 sheets) filo pastry

2 tbsp butter, melted

1 To make the filling, heat the oil and butter in a frying pan. Add the potatoes and leek and fry, stirring constantly, for 2–3 minutes. Add the garlic and spices, okra, mushrooms, tomatoes, and tofu and season to taste with salt and pepper. Cook, stirring, for 5–7 minutes, or until tender.

2 Lay the pastry out on a chopping board and brush each individual sheet with melted butter. Place 3 sheets on top of one another; repeat to make 4 stacks.

3 Spoon a quarter of the filling along the centre of each stack and brush the edges with melted butter. Fold the short edges in and roll up lengthways to form a cigar shape. Brush the outside with melted butter. Place the strudels on a greased baking tray.

4 Cook in a preheated oven, 190°C/375°F/Gas Mark 5, for 20 minutes, or until golden brown and crisp. Transfer to a warm serving dish and serve immediately.

Vegetable Hotpot

In this recipe, a variety of vegetables are cooked under a layer of potatoes, topped with cheese and cooked until golden brown.

NUTRITIONAL INFORMATION

Calories	279	Sugars	........12g
Protein	........10g	Fat	...........11g
Carbohydrate	...34g	Saturates	.......4g

   25 mins   1 hr

SERVES 4

I N G R E D I E N T S

600 g/1 lb 5 oz potatoes, thinly sliced

2 tbsp vegetable oil

1 red onion, halved and sliced

1 leek, sliced

2 garlic cloves, crushed

1 carrot, cut into chunks

100 g/3½ oz broccoli florets

100 g/3½ oz cauliflower florets

2 small turnips, quartered

1 tbsp plain flour

700 ml/1¼ pints vegetable stock

150 ml/5 fl oz dry cider

1 eating apple, cored and sliced

2 tbsp chopped fresh sage

pinch of cayenne pepper

50 g/1¾ oz Cheddar cheese, grated

salt and pepper

1 Cook the potato slices in a saucepan of boiling water for 10 minutes. Drain thoroughly and reserve.

2 Heat the oil in a flameproof casserole. Add the onion, leek and garlic and sauté, stirring occasionally, for 2–3 minutes. Add the remaining vegetables and cook, stirring constantly, for a further 3–4 minutes.

3 Stir in the flour and cook for 1 minute. Gradually add the stock and cider and bring to the boil. Add the apple, sage and cayenne pepper and season well. Remove from the heat and transfer the vegetables to an ovenproof dish.

4 Arrange the potato slices on top of the vegetable mixture to cover.

5 Sprinkle the cheese on top of the potato slices and cook in a preheated oven, 190°C/375°F/Gas Mark 5, for 30–35 minutes or until the potato is golden brown and beginning to go crisp around the edges. Serve immediately.

Vegetable Biryani

The Biryani originated in the north of India and was a dish reserved for festivals. The vegetables are marinated in a yogurt-based marinade.

NUTRITIONAL INFORMATION

Calories . . . . . . .449 Sugars 18g
Protein . . . . .12g Fat 12g
Carbohydrate . . .79g Saturates 6g

15 mins, plus 2 hrs to marinate   1 hr 5 mins

SERVES 4

INGREDIENTS

300 g/10½ oz potato, cubed

100 g/3½ oz baby carrots

50 g/1¾ oz okra, thickly sliced

2 celery sticks, sliced

75 g/2¾ oz baby button mushrooms, halved

1 aubergine, halved and sliced

300 ml/10 fl oz natural yogurt

1 tbsp grated fresh root ginger

2 large onions, grated

4 garlic cloves, crushed

1 tsp turmeric

1 tbsp curry powder

2 tbsp butter

2 onions, sliced

225 g/8 oz basmati rice

chopped fresh coriander, to garnish

1 Cook the potato cubes, carrots and okra in a pan of boiling salted water for 7–8 minutes. Drain well and place in a large bowl. Mix with the celery, mushrooms and aubergine.

2 Mix the natural yogurt, ginger, grated onions, garlic, turmeric and curry powder and spoon over the vegetables.

Set aside in a cool place to marinate for at least 2 hours.

3 Heat the butter in a heavy-based frying pan. Add the sliced onions and cook over a medium heat for 5–6 minutes, until golden brown. Remove a few onions from the pan and reserve for the garnish.

4 Cook the rice in a large pan of boiling water for 7 minutes. Drain thoroughly and set aside.

5 Add the marinated vegetables to the onions and cook for 10 minutes.

6 Put half of the rice in a 2-litre/3½-pint casserole dish. Spoon the vegetables on top and cover with the remaining rice. Cover and cook in a preheated oven, 190°C/375°F/Gas Mark 5, for 20–25 minutes, or until the rice is tender.

7 Spoon the biryani on to a serving plate, garnish with the reserved onions and coriander and serve.

Cauliflower Bake

The red of the tomatoes is a great contrast to the cauliflower and herbs, making this dish appealing to both the eye and the palate.

NUTRITIONAL INFORMATION

Calories . . . . . . .305 Sugars 9g
Protein . . . . .15g Fat 14g
Carbohydrate . . .31g Saturates 6g

 10 mins   ⏱ 40 mins

SERVES 4

INGREDIENTS

500 g/1 lb 2 oz cauliflower, broken into
  florets

600 g/1 lb 5 oz potatoes, cubed

100 g/3½ oz cherry tomatoes

SAUCE

2 tbsp butter or margarine

1 leek, sliced

1 garlic clove, crushed

3 tbsp plain flour

300 ml/10 fl oz milk

75 g/2¾ oz mixed cheese, such as Cheddar,
  Parmesan and Gruyère, grated

½ tsp paprika

2 tbsp chopped flat leaf parsley

salt and pepper

chopped parsley, to garnish

1 Cook the cauliflower in a saucepan of boiling water for 10 minutes. Drain well and reserve. Meanwhile, cook the potatoes in a pan of boiling water for 10 minutes, drain and reserve.

2 To make the sauce, melt the butter or margarine in a saucepan and sauté the leek and garlic for 1 minute. Stir in the flour and cook, stirring constantly, for 1 minute. Remove the pan from the heat and gradually stir in the milk, 50 g/ 1³/₄ oz of the cheese, the paprika and parsley. Return the pan to the heat and bring to the boil, stirring constantly. Season with salt and pepper to taste.

3 Spoon the cauliflower into a deep ovenproof dish. Add the cherry tomatoes and top with the potatoes. Pour the sauce over the potatoes and sprinkle on the remaining cheese.

4 Cook in a preheated oven, 180°C/ 350°F/Gas Mark 4, for 20 minutes, or until the vegetables are cooked through and the cheese is golden brown and bubbling. Garnish and serve immediately.

VARIATION
This dish could be made with broccoli instead of the cauliflower as an alternative.

Gnocchi with Tomato Sauce

Freshly made potato gnocchi are delicious, especially when they are topped with a fragrant tomato sauce.

NUTRITIONAL INFORMATION

Calories 216   Sugars 5g
Protein . . . . .5g   Fat 6g
Carbohydrate . . .39g   Saturates 1g

 30 mins   45 mins

SERVES 4

INGREDIENTS

350 g/12 oz floury potatoes, halved

75 g/2¾ oz self-raising flour, plus extra for rolling out

2 tsp dried oregano

2 tbsp oil

1 large onion, chopped

2 garlic cloves, chopped

400 g/14 oz canned chopped tomatoes

½ vegetable stock cube dissolved in 100 ml/3½ fl oz boiling water

2 tbsp fresh basil, shredded, plus whole leaves to garnish

salt and pepper

Parmesan cheese, freshly grated, to serve

1 Bring a large saucepan of water to the boil. Add the potatoes and cook for 12–15 minutes or until tender. Drain and leave to cool.

2 Peel and then mash the potatoes with the salt and pepper, sifted flour and oregano. Mix together with your hands to form a dough.

3 Heat the oil in a pan. Add the onions and garlic and cook for 3–4 minutes. Add the tomatoes and stock and cook, uncovered, for 10 minutes. Season with salt and pepper to taste.

4 Roll the potato dough into a sausage about 2.5 cm/1 inch in diameter. Cut the sausage into 2.5-cm/1-inch lengths. Flour your hands, then press a fork into each piece to create a series of ridges on one side and the indent of your index finger on the other.

5 Bring a large saucepan of water to the boil and cook the gnocchi, in batches, for 2–3 minutes. They should rise to the surface when cooked. Drain well and keep warm.

6 Stir the basil into the tomato sauce and pour over the gnocchi. Garnish with basil leaves and season with pepper to taste. Sprinkle with Parmesan and serve at once.

VARIATION
The gnocchi can also be served with a pesto sauce made from fresh basil leaves, pine nuts, garlic, olive oil and pecorino or Parmesan cheese.

Fish Dishes

There is no denying that fish and potatoes are a terrific combination. In these recipes potatoes are used in a variety of ways to enhance the fish. They are used to form a crispy coating for cod, and mashed to make the basis of fish cakes and fritters. They are sliced to form part of a

layered pie, and sautéd with shallots to create the perfect accompaniment to a red mullet wrapped in parma ham. These recipes also include some interesting flavours from France, such as Cotriade, a satisfying stew of fish and vegetables flavoured with herbs. For health-conscious cooks, the nutritious value of these dishes is unbeatable.

Fishcakes & Piquant Sauce

The combination of pink- and white-fleshed fish, with a tasty tomato sauce, transforms the humble fish into something a bit special.

NUTRITIONAL INFORMATION

Calories ....334 Sugars 7g
Protein ....31g Fat 7g
Carbohydrate ...37g Saturates 1g

30 mins, plus 1 hr chilling time

55 mins

SERVES 4

INGREDIENTS

450 g/1 lb potatoes, diced

225 g/8 oz trout fillet

225 g/8 oz haddock fillet

1 bay leaf

425 ml/15 fl oz fish stock

2 tbsp low-fat natural fromage frais

4 tbsp snipped fresh chives

75 g/2¾ oz dry white breadcrumbs

1 tbsp sunflower oil

salt and pepper

snipped fresh chives, to garnish

lemon wedges and salad leaves,
   to serve

PIQUANT SAUCE

200 ml/7 fl oz passata

4 tbsp dry white wine

4 tbsp low-fat natural yogurt

chilli powder

2 Meanwhile, place the fish in a pan with the bay leaf and fish stock. Bring to the boil and simmer for about 7–8 minutes until tender.

3 Remove the fish with a slotted spoon and flake the flesh away from the skin. Gently mix the cooked fish with the potato, fromage frais, chives and seasoning. Leave to cool, then cover and leave to chill for 1 hour.

4 Sprinkle the breadcrumbs on to a plate. Divide the fish mixture into eight and form each portion into a patty, about 7.5 cm/3 inches in diameter. Press each fishcake into the breadcrumbs, coating all over.

5 Brush a frying pan with oil and fry the fishcakes for 6 minutes. Turn the fishcakes over and cook for a further 5–6 minutes until golden. Drain on kitchen paper and keep warm.

6 To make the sauce, heat the passata and wine. Season, remove from the heat and stir in the yogurt. Return briefly to the heat then transfer to a small serving bowl and sprinkle with chilli powder. Garnish the fishcakes with chives and serve with lemon wedges, salad leaves and the sauce.

1 Place the potatoes in a saucepan and cover with water. Bring to the boil and cook for about 10 minutes or until the potatoes are tender. Drain thoroughly and mash well.

Potato-topped Cod

This simple dish has a spicy breadcrumb topping over layers of cod and potatoes. It is cooked in the oven until crisp and golden.

NUTRITIONAL INFORMATION

Calories	118	Sugars	.......1.0g
Protein	........9.8g	Fat	..........4.4g
Carbohydrate	..10.5g	Saturates	.....2.6g

 5–10 mins   35 mins

SERVES 4

I N G R E D I E N T S

5 tbsp butter

900 g/2 lb waxy potatoes, sliced

1 large onion, finely chopped

1 tsp wholegrain mustard

1 tsp garam masala

pinch of chilli powder

1 tbsp chopped fresh dill

75 g/2¾ oz fresh breadcrumbs

700g /1 lb 9 oz cod fillet

50 g/1¾ oz Gruyère cheese, grated

salt and pepper

fresh dill sprigs, to garnish

1 Melt half of the butter in a frying pan. Add the potatoes and fry for 5 minutes, turning until they are browned all over. Remove the potatoes from the pan with a perforated spoon.

2 Add the remaining butter to the frying pan and stir in the onion, mustard, garam masala, chilli powder, dill and breadcrumbs. Cook for 1–2 minutes, stirring and mixing well.

3 Layer half of the potatoes in the base of an ovenproof dish and place the

cod fillets on top. Cover the cod fillets with the rest of the potato slices. Season to taste with salt and pepper.

4 Spoon the spicy mixture from the frying pan over the potato and sprinkle with the grated cheese.

5 Cook in a preheated oven, 200°C/400°F/Gas Mark 6, for 20–25 minutes or until the topping is golden and crisp and the fish is cooked through. Remove from the oven, garnish with fresh dill sprigs and serve at once.

COOK'S TIP

This dish is ideal served with baked vegetables, which can be cooked in the oven at the same time.

Layered Fish & Potato Pie

This is a really delicious and filling dish. Layers of potato slices and mixed fish are cooked in a creamy sauce and topped with grated cheese.

NUTRITIONAL INFORMATION

Calories 116	Sugars 1.9g
Protein 6.2g	Fat 6.1g
Carbohydrate . . .9.7g	Saturates 3.8g

 10 mins   55 mins

SERVES 4

INGREDIENTS

900 g/2 lb waxy potatoes, sliced

5 tbsp butter

1 red onion, halved and sliced

5 tbsp plain flour

450 ml/16 fl oz milk

150 ml/5 fl oz double cream

225 g/8 oz smoked haddock fillet, cubed

225 g/8 oz cod fillet, cubed

1 red pepper, diced

125 g/4½ oz broccoli florets

50 g/1¾ oz Parmesan cheese, freshly grated

salt and pepper

1 Cook the sliced potatoes in a saucepan of boiling water for 10 minutes. Drain and set aside.

2 Meanwhile, melt the butter in a saucepan, add the onion and fry gently for 3–4 minutes.

3 Add the flour and cook for 1 minute. Blend in the milk and cream and bring to the boil, stirring until the sauce has thickened.

4 Arrange half of the potato slices in the base of a shallow ovenproof dish.

5 Add the fish, red pepper and broccoli to the sauce and cook over a low heat for 10 minutes. Season with salt and pepper, then spoon the mixture over the potatoes in the dish.

6 Arrange the remaining potato slices in a layer over the fish mixture. Sprinkle the Parmesan cheese over the top.

7 Cook in a preheated oven, 180°C/350°F/Gas Mark 4, for 30 minutes or until the potatoes are cooked and the top is golden.

COOK'S TIP

Choose your favourite combination of fish, adding salmon or various shellfish for special occasions.

Tuna & Cheese Quiche

The base for this quiche is made from mashed potato instead of pastry, giving a softer textured case for the tasty tuna filling.

NUTRITIONAL INFORMATION

Calories ....383 Sugars 5g
Protein ....25g Fat 15g
Carbohydrate ...40g Saturates 6g

 20 mins 🕐 1 hr

SERVES 4

INGREDIENTS

450 g/1 lb floury potatoes, diced

2 tbsp butter

6 tbsp plain flour

FILLING

1 tbsp vegetable oil

1 shallot, chopped

1 garlic clove, crushed

1 red pepper, diced

175g/6 oz drained canned tuna in brine

50 g/1¾ oz drained canned sweetcorn

150 ml/5 fl oz skimmed milk

3 eggs, beaten

1 tbsp chopped fresh dill

50 g/1¾ oz mature low-fat cheese, grated

salt and pepper

TO GARNISH

fresh dill sprigs

lemon wedges

1 Cook the potatoes in a pan of boiling water for 10 minutes or until tender. Drain and mash the potatoes. Add the butter and flour and mix to form a dough.

2 Knead the potato dough on a floured surface and press the mixture into a 20-cm/8-inch flan tin. Prick the base with a fork. Line with baking paper and baking beans and bake blind in a preheated oven, 200°C/400°F/Gas Mark 6, for 20 minutes.

3 Heat the oil in a frying pan, add the shallot, garlic and pepper and fry gently for 5 minutes. Drain well and spoon the mixture into the flan case. Flake the tuna and arrange it over the top with the sweetcorn.

4 In a bowl, mix the milk, eggs and chopped dill and season.

5 Pour the egg and dill mixture into the flan case and sprinkle the grated cheese on top.

6 Bake in the oven for 20 minutes or until the filling has set. Garnish the quiche with fresh dill and lemon wedges. Serve with mixed vegetables or salad.

Fish & Potato Pie

This flavoursome and colourful fish pie is perfect for a light supper. The addition of smoked salmon gives it a touch of luxury.

NUTRITIONAL INFORMATION

Calories	523	Sugars	........15g
Protein	........58g	Fat	...........6g
Carbohydrate	...63g	Saturates	......2g

15 mins   1 hr

SERVES 4

INGREDIENTS

900 g/2 lb smoked haddock or
 cod fillets

600 ml/1 pint skimmed milk

2 bay leaves

115 g/4 oz button mushrooms, quartered

115 g/4 oz frozen peas

115 g/4 oz frozen sweetcorn kernels

675 g/1½ lb potatoes, diced

5 tbsp low-fat natural yogurt

4 tbsp chopped fresh parsley

55 g/2 oz smoked salmon, sliced into
 thin strips

3 tbsp cornflour

25 g/1 oz smoked cheese, grated

salt and pepper

1 Preheat the oven to 200°C/400°F/Gas Mark 6. Place the fish in a pan and add the milk and bay leaves. Bring to the boil, cover and then simmer for 5 minutes.

2 Add the mushrooms, peas and sweetcorn, bring back to a simmer, cover and cook for 5–7 minutes. Leave to cool.

3 Place the potatoes in a saucepan, cover with water, boil and cook for 8 minutes. Drain well and mash with a fork or a potato masher. Stir in the yogurt, parsley and seasoning. Set aside.

4 Using a slotted spoon, remove the fish from the pan. Flake the cooked fish away from the skin and place in an ovenproof gratin dish. Reserve the cooking liquid.

5 Drain the vegetables, reserving the cooking liquid, and gently stir into the fish with the salmon strips.

6 Blend a little cooking liquid into the cornflour to make a paste. Transfer the rest of the liquid to a saucepan and add the paste. Heat through, stirring, until thickened. Discard the bay leaves and season to taste. Pour the sauce over the fish and vegetables and mix. Cover the fish with the mashed potato, sprinkle with cheese and bake for 25–30 minutes.

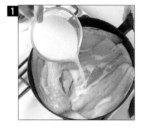

COOK'S TIP

If possible, use smoked haddock or cod that has not been dyed bright yellow or artificially flavoured to give the illusion of having been smoked.

Salt Cod Fritters

Mediterranean cooks have always made the most of dried salted cod, once the only source of cod during harsh winter months.

NUTRITIONAL INFORMATION

Calories 300	Sugars 1g	
Protein 16g	Fat 22g	
Carbohydrate 11g	Saturates 3g	

30 mins, plus 48 hrs soaking time   45 mins

SERVES 6

I N G R E D I E N T S

450 g/1 lb salt cod

350 g/12 oz floury baking potatoes

1 tbsp olive oil, plus extra for frying

1 onion, very finely chopped

1 garlic clove, crushed

4 tbsp very finely chopped fresh parsley or coriander

1 tbsp capers in brine, drained and finely chopped (optional)

1 small egg, lightly beaten

salt and pepper

aïoli, to serve

1 Break the salt cod into pieces and place in a bowl. Add enough water to cover and leave for 48 hours, changing the water 4 times.

2 Drain the salt cod, then cook in boiling water for 20-25 minutes until tender. Drain, then remove all the skin and bones. Using a fork, flake the fish into fine pieces that still retain some texture.

3 Meanwhile, boil the potatoes in their skins until tender. Drain, peel and mash in a large bowl. Set aside.

4 Heat 1 tablespoon of the oil in a frying pan. Add the onion and garlic and fry for 5 minutes, stirring, until tender but not brown. Remove with a slotted spoon and drain on kitchen paper.

5 Stir the salt cod, onion and garlic into the mashed potatoes. Stir in the parsley and capers, if using. Season generously with pepper.

6 Stir in the beaten egg. Cover and chill for 30 minutes, then adjust the seasoning.

7 Heat 5 cm/2 inches oil in a frying pan to 180°–190°C/350–375°F, or until a cube of bread browns in 30 seconds. Drop tablespoonfuls of the salt-cod mixture into the hot oil and fry for about 8 minutes or until golden brown and set. Do not fry more than 6 at a time because the oil will become too cold and the fritters will become soggy. You will get 18-20 fritters.

8 Drain the fritters on kitchen paper. Serve at once with aïoli for dipping. Garnish with parsley.

Cotriade

This is a rich French stew of fish and vegetables, flavoured with saffron and herbs. The fish and vegetables, and the soup, are served separately.

NUTRITIONAL INFORMATION

Calories 81	Sugars 0.9g
Protein 7.4g	Fat 3.9g
Carbohydrate . . .3.8g	Saturates 1.1g

15 mins | 40 mins

SERVES 6

INGREDIENTS

large pinch saffron

600 ml/1 pint hot fish stock

1 tbsp olive oil

2 tbsp butter

1 onion, sliced

2 garlic cloves, chopped

1 leek, sliced

1 small fennel bulb, finely sliced

450 g/1 lb potatoes, cut into chunks

150 ml/5 fl oz dry white wine

1 tbsp fresh thyme leaves

2 bay leaves

4 ripe tomatoes, skinned and chopped

2 lb mixed fish such as haddock, hake, mackerel, red or gray mullet, roughly chopped

2 tbsp chopped fresh parsley

salt and pepper

crusty bread, to serve

1 Using a mortar and pestle, crush the saffron and add to the fish stock. Stir the mixture and leave to infuse for at least 10 minutes.

2 In a large saucepan, heat the oil and butter together. Add the onion and cook gently for 4–5 minutes until softened. Add the garlic, leek, fennel and potatoes. Cover and cook for an additional 10–15 minutes until the vegetables are softened.

3 Add the wine and simmer rapidly for 3–4 minutes until reduced by half. Add the thyme, bay leaves and tomatoes and stir well. Add the saffron-infused fish stock. Bring to the boil, cover and simmer gently for 15 minutes until the vegetables are tender.

4 Add the fish, return to the boil and simmer for a further 3–4 minutes until all the fish is tender. Add the parsley and season to taste. Using a slotted spoon, remove the fish and vegetables to a warmed serving dish. Serve the soup with plenty of crusty bread.

VARIATION

Once the fish and vegetables have been cooked, you could process the soup and pass it through a sieve to give a smooth fish soup.

Grilled Red Mullet

Try to get small red mullet for this dish. If you can only get larger fish, serve one to each person and increase the cooking time accordingly.

10 mins   20 mins

SERVES 4

I N G R E D I E N T S

1 lemon, thinly sliced

2 garlic cloves, crushed

4 sprigs fresh flat-leaf parsley

4 sprigs fresh thyme

8 leaves fresh sage

2 large shallots, sliced

8 small red mullet, cleaned

8 slices Parma ham

salt and pepper

SAUTÉ POTATOES AND SHALLOTS

4 tbsp olive oil

900 g/2 lb potatoes, diced

8 whole garlic cloves, unpeeled

12 small whole shallots

FOR THE DRESSING

4 tbsp olive oil

1 tbsp lemon juice

1 tbsp chopped fresh flat-leaf parsley

1 tbsp chopped fresh chives

salt and pepper

1 For the sauté potatoes and shallots, heat the olive oil in a large frying pan and add the potatoes, garlic cloves and shallots. Cook gently, stirring regularly, for 12–15 minutes until they are golden, crisp and tender.

2 Meanwhile, divide the lemon slices, halved if necessary, garlic, parsley, thyme, sage and shallots between the cavities of the fish. Season well. Wrap a slice of Parma ham around each fish. Secure with a cocktail stick.

3 Arrange the fish on a grill pan and cook under a preheated hot grill for 5–6 minutes on each side until tender.

4 To make the dressing, mix together the oil and lemon juice with the finely chopped parsley and chives. Season with salt and pepper to taste.

5 Divide the potatoes and shallots among four serving plates and top each with the fish. Drizzle around the dressing and serve immediately.

 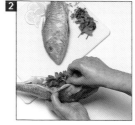 

Poached Rainbow Trout

This colourful, flavoursome dish is served cold, and therefore makes a lovely summer lunch or supper dish.

NUTRITIONAL INFORMATION

Calories 99   Sugars 1.1g
Protein . . . . .5.7g   Fat 6.3g
Carbohydrate . . .3.7g   Saturates 1g

10 mins, plus 15 mins cooling time   1 hr 5 mins

SERVES 4

INGREDIENTS

1.3 kg/3 lb rainbow trout fillet, cleaned

700 g/1 lb 9 oz new potatoes

3 spring onions, finely chopped

1 egg, hard-boiled and chopped

COURT-BOUILLON

850 ml/1½ pints cold water

850 ml/1½ pints dry white wine

3 tbsp white wine vinegar

2 large carrots, roughly chopped

1 onion, roughly chopped

2 celery sticks, roughly chopped

2 leeks, roughly chopped

2 garlic cloves, roughly chopped

2 fresh bay leaves

4 sprigs fresh parsley

4 sprigs fresh thyme

6 black peppercorns

1 tsp salt

WATERCRESS MAYONNAISE

1 egg yolk

1 tsp Dijon mustard

1 tsp white wine vinegar

2 oz watercress leaves, chopped

225 ml/8 fl oz light olive oil

salt and pepper

1 First make the court-bouillon. Place all the ingredients in a large saucepan and bring slowly to the boil. Cover and simmer gently for about 30 minutes. Strain the liquid through a fine sieve into a clean pan. Bring to the boil again and simmer fast, uncovered, for 15–20 minutes until the court-bouillon is reduced to 600 ml/1 pint.

2 Place the trout in a large frying pan. Add the court-bouillon and bring slowly to the boil. Remove from the heat and leave the fish in the poaching liquid to go cold.

3 Meanwhile, make the watercress mayonnaise. Put the egg yolk, mustard, wine vinegar, watercress and seasoning into a food processor or blender and blend for 30 seconds until foaming. Begin adding the olive oil, drop by drop, until the mixture begins to thicken. Continue adding the oil in a slow steady stream until it is all incorporated. Add a little hot water if the mixture seems too thick. Season to taste and set aside.

4 Cook the potatoes in plenty of boiling salted water for 12–15 minutes until soft and tender. Drain well and refresh them under cold running water. Set the potatoes aside until cold.

5 When the potatoes are cold, cut them in half if they are very large, and toss thoroughly with the watercress mayonnaise, finely chopped spring onions and hard-boiled egg.

6 Carefully lift the fish from the poaching liquid and drain on kitchen paper. Carefully pull the skin away from each of the trout and serve immediately with the potato salad.

Smoked Fish Pie

What cookbook would be complete without a fish pie? This is a classic version with smoked fish, prawns and vegetables.

NUTRITIONAL INFORMATION

Calories ....562 Sugars 9g
Protein ....42g Fat 29g
Carbohydrate ...35g Saturates 16g

 10 mins   🕐 1 hr 30 mins

SERVES 6

INGREDIENTS

2 tbsp olive oil

1 onion, finely chopped

1 leek, thinly sliced

1 carrot, diced

1 celery stick, diced

115 g/4 oz button mushrooms, halved

grated rind 1 lemon

350 g/12 oz skinless, boneless smoked cod or haddock fillet, cubed

350 g/12 oz skinless, boneless white fish such as haddock, hake or monkfish, cubed

8 oz cooked peeled prawns

2 tbsp chopped fresh parsley

1 tbsp chopped fresh dill

SAUCE

4 tbsp butter

4 tbsp plain flour

1 tsp mustard powder

600 ml/1 pint milk

85 g/3 oz Gruyère cheese, grated

TOPPING

675 g/1½ lb potatoes, unpeeled

4 tbsp butter, melted

25 g/1 oz Gruyère cheese, grated

salt and pepper

1 For the sauce, heat the butter in a large saucepan and when melted, add the flour and mustard powder. Stir until smooth and cook over a very low heat for 2 minutes without colouring. Slowly beat in the milk until smooth. Simmer gently for 2 minutes then stir in the cheese until smooth. Remove from the heat and put some clingfilm over the surface of the sauce to prevent a skin from forming. Set aside.

2 Meanwhile, for the topping, boil the whole potatoes in plenty of salted water for 15 minutes. Drain well and set aside until cool enough to handle.

3 Heat the olive oil in a clean pan and add the onion. Cook for 5 minutes until softened. Add the sliced leek, the diced carrot and celery and the mushrooms and cook for a further 10 minutes until the vegetables have softened. Stir in the lemon rind and cook briefly.

4 Add the softened vegetables with the fish, prawns, parsley and dill to the sauce. Season to taste and transfer to a greased 1.75-litre/3-pint casserole dish.

5 Peel the cooled potatoes and grate them coarsely. Mix with the melted butter. Cover the filling with the grated potato and sprinkle with the grated Gruyère cheese.

6 Cover loosely with foil and bake in a preheated oven at 200°C/400°F/Gas Mark 6, for 30 minutes. Remove the foil and bake for an additional 30 minutes until the topping is tender and golden and the filling is bubbling. Serve immediately with your favourite selection of vegetables.

Herring & Potato Pie

The combination of herrings, apples and potatoes is popular throughout northern Europe. In salads, one often sees the addition of beetroots.

NUTRITIONAL INFORMATION

Calories ....574 Sugars 10g
Protein ....17g Fat 36g
Carbohydrate ...48g Saturates 19g

15–20 mins   1 hr 5 mins

SERVES 4

INGREDIENTS

1 tbsp Dijon mustard

115 g/4 oz butter, softened

450 g/1 lb herrings, filleted

750 g/1 lb 10 oz potatoes

1 large onion, sliced

2 cooking apples, sliced thinly

1 tsp chopped fresh sage

600 ml/1 pint hot fish stock

50 g/1¾ oz crustless ciabatta, made into breadcrumbs

salt and pepper

parsley sprigs, to garnish

1 Mix the mustard with 25 g/1 oz of the butter until smooth. Spread this mixture over the cut sides of of the herring fillets. Season and roll up the fillets. Set aside. Generously grease a 2.2-litre/4-pint pie dish with some of the remaining butter.

2 Thinly slice the potatoes, using a mandolin if possible. Blanch for 3 minutes in plenty of boiling, salted water until just tender. Drain well, refresh under cold water and then pat dry.

3 Heat 25 g/1 oz of the remaining butter in a frying pan and add the onion. Cook gently for 8–10 minutes until soft but not coloured. Remove from the heat and set aside.

4 Put half the potato slices into the bottom of the pie dish with some seasoning then add half the apple and half the onion. Put the herring fillets on top of the onion and sprinkle with the sage. Repeat the layers in reverse order, ending with potato. Season well and add enough hot stock to come halfway up the sides of the dish.

5 Melt the remaining butter and stir in the breadcrumbs until well combined. Sprinkle the breadcrumbs over the pie. Bake in a preheated oven, 190°C/375° F/Gas Mark 5, for 40–50 minutes until the breadcrumbs are golden and the herrings are cooked through. Serve garnished with parsley.

VARIATION

If herrings are unavailable, substitute mackerel or sardines.

Luxury Fish Pie

This is a fish pie for pushing out the boat! Try piping the potato topping decoratively over the pie – it looks wonderful when baked.

NUTRITIONAL INFORMATION

Calories . . . . . . .863 Sugars 5g
Protein . . . . .66g Fat 41g
Carbohydrate . . .60g Saturates 24g

 10 mins   1 hr 10 mins

SERVES 4

I N G R E D I E N T S

85 g/3 oz butter

3 shallots, finely chopped

115 g/4 oz button mushrooms, halved

2 tbsp dry white wine

900 g/2 lb live mussels, scrubbed and bearded

1 quantity court-bouillon (see Poached Rainbow Trout, page 210)

300 g/10½ oz monkfish fillet, cubed

300 g/10½ oz skinless cod fillet, cubed

300 g/10½ oz skinless lemon sole fillet, cubed

4 oz tiger prawns, peeled

2½ tbsp plain flour

3 tbsp double cream

P O T A T O   T O P P I N G

1.5 kg/3 lb 5 oz floury potatoes, cut into chunks

4 tbsp butter

2 egg yolks

125 ml/4 fl oz milk

pinch freshly grated nutmeg

salt and pepper

fresh parsley, to garnish

1 For the filling, melt 25 g/1 oz of the butter in a frying pan, add the shallots and cook for 5 minutes until softened. Add the mushrooms and cook over a high heat for 2 minutes. Add the wine and simmer until the liquid has evaporated. Transfer to a 1.5-litre/2¾-pint shallow ovenproof dish and set aside.

2 Put the mussels into a large saucepan with just the water clinging to their shells and cook, covered, over a high heat for 3–4 minutes until all the mussels have opened. Discard any that remain closed. Drain, reserving the cooking liquid. When cool enough to handle, remove the mussels from their shells and add to the mushrooms.

3 Bring the court-bouillon to a boil and add the monkfish. Poach gently for 2 minutes before adding the cod, sole and prawns. Poach for a further 2 minutes. Remove the fish with a slotted spoon and add to the mussels and mushrooms.

4 Melt the remaining butter in a saucepan and add the flour. Stir until smooth and cook for 2 minutes without colouring. Gradually, stir in the hot court-bouillon and mussel cooking liquid until smooth and thickened. Add the cream and simmer gently for 15 minutes, stirring. Season to taste and pour over the fish.

5 Meanwhile, make the topping. Boil the potatoes in plenty of salted water for 15–20 minutes until tender. Drain well and mash with the butter, egg yolks, milk, nutmeg and seasoning. Pipe over the fish, or spread with a spatula, and roughen the surface of the topping with a fork.

6 Bake the finished fish pie in a preheated oven at 200°C/400° F/Gas Mark 6, for 30 minutes until golden and bubbling. Serve straight from the oven, piping hot with a garnish of fresh parsley.

Poultry & Meat

This chapter contains a wide selection of delicious main meal dishes. The potato is the main ingredient in the majority of these recipes, but there are also ideas for adding meat, poultry, fish and vegetables, so that there is sure to be something for everyone. The recipes come from all around the world – try Potato Ravioli or Potato and Lamb Kofta. There are also hearty dishes including Creamy Chicken and Potato Casserole, and Lamb Hotpot. Whatever the occasion, you are sure to find something here to entice you.

Baked Southern-Style Chicken

Traditionally, this dish is deep-fried, but the low-fat version is just as mouthwatering. Serve with chunky potato wedge chips.

NUTRITIONAL INFORMATION

Calories 361   Sugars 2g
Protein . . . . .24g   Fat 8g
Carbohydrate . . .51g   Saturates 2g

 10 mins   35 mins

SERVES 4

I N G R E D I E N T S

4 small baking potatoes

1 tbsp sunflower oil

2 tsp coarse sea salt

2 tbsp plain flour

pinch of cayenne pepper

½ tsp paprika pepper

½ tsp dried thyme

8 chicken drumsticks, skin removed

1 medium egg, beaten

2 tbsp cold water

6 tbsp dry white breadcrumbs

salt and pepper

T O   S E R V E

low-fat coleslaw salad

sweetcorn relish

1 Preheat the oven to 200°C/400°F/Gas Mark 6. Wash and scrub the potatoes and cut each into 8 equal portions. Place in a clean plastic bag and add the oil. Seal and shake well to coat.

2 Arrange the potato wedges, skin side down, on a non-stick baking tray, sprinkle over the sea salt and bake in the oven for 30–35 minutes until they are tender and golden.

3 Meanwhile, mix the flour, spices, thyme and seasoning together on a plate. Press the chicken drumsticks into the seasoned flour to lightly coat.

4 On one plate mix together the egg and water. On another plate sprinkle the breadcrumbs. Dip the chicken drumsticks first into the egg and then coat them in the breadcrumbs. Place on a non-stick baking tray.

5 Bake the chicken drumsticks alongside the potato wedges for 30 minutes, turning after 15 minutes, until both potatoes and chicken are tender and cooked through.

6 Drain the potato wedges thoroughly on absorbent kitchen paper to remove any excess fat and serve with the chicken, accompanied with low-fat coleslaw and sweetcorn relish.

Chicken & Banana Cakes

Potato cakes are a great favourite. In this recipe the potatoes are combined with minced chicken and mashed banana.

NUTRITIONAL INFORMATION

Calories 439   Sugars 11g
Protein ....22g   Fat 23g
Carbohydrate ...39g   Saturates 10g

 5–10 mins   25–30 mins

SERVES 4

INGREDIENTS

450 g/1 lb floury potatoes, diced

225 g/8 oz minced chicken

1 large banana

2 tbsp plain flour

1 tsp lemon juice

1 onion, finely chopped

2 tbsp chopped fresh sage

2 tbsp butter

2 tbsp vegetable oil

150 ml/5 fl oz single cream

150 ml/5 fl oz chicken stock

salt and pepper

fresh sage leaves, to garnish

1 Cook the diced potatoes in a saucepan of boiling water for 10 minutes until cooked through. Drain and mash the potatoes until smooth. Stir in the minced chicken.

2 Mash the banana and add it to the potato with the flour, lemon juice, onion and half of the chopped sage. Season well and stir the mixture together.

3 Divide the mixture into 8 equal portions. With lightly floured hands, shape each portion into a round patty.

4 Heat the butter and oil in a frying pan, add the potato cakes and cook for 12–15 minutes or until cooked through, turning once. Remove from the pan and keep warm.

5 Stir the cream and stock into the pan with the remaining chopped sage. Cook over a low heat for 2–3 minutes.

6 Arrange the potato cakes on a serving plate, garnish with fresh sage leaves and serve with the cream and sage sauce.

COOK'S TIP
Do not boil the sauce once the cream has been added as it will curdle. Cook it gently over a very low heat.

Potato, Leek & Chicken Pie

This pie has an attractive filo pastry case that has a 'ruffled' top made with strips of the pastry brushed with melted butter.

NUTRITIONAL INFORMATION

Calories 543   Sugars 7g
Protein ....21g   Fat 27g
Carbohydrate ...56g   Saturates 16g

10 mins   1 hr 15 mins

SERVES 4

INGREDIENTS

225 g/8 oz waxy potatoes, cubed

5 tbsp butter

1 skinned chicken breast fillet, about 175 g/6 oz, cubed

1 leek, sliced

150 g/5½ oz chestnut mushrooms, sliced

2½ tbsp plain flour

300 ml/10 fl oz milk

1 tbsp Dijon mustard

2 tbsp chopped fresh sage

225 g/8 oz filo pastry, thawed if frozen

3 tbsp butter, melted

salt and pepper

1 Cook the potato cubes in a saucepan of boiling water for 5 minutes. Drain and set aside.

2 Melt the butter in a frying pan and cook the chicken cubes for 5 minutes or until browned all over.

3 Add the leek and mushrooms and cook for 3 minutes, stirring. Stir in the flour and cook for 1 minute. Gradually add the milk and bring to the boil. Add the mustard, sage and potato cubes, then leave the mixture to simmer for 10 minutes.

4 Meanwhile, line a deep pie dish with half of the sheets of filo pastry. Spoon the sauce into the dish and cover with one sheet of pastry. Brush the pastry with butter and lay another sheet on top. Brush this sheet with butter.

5 Cut the remaining filo pastry into strips and fold them on to the top of the pie to create a ruffled effect. Brush the strips with the melted butter and cook in a preheated oven 180°C/350°F/Gas Mark 4, for 45 minutes or until golden brown and crisp. Serve hot.

COOK'S TIP

If the top of the pie starts to brown too quickly, cover it with foil halfway through the cooking time to allow the pastry base to cook through without the top burning.

Quick Chicken Bake

This recipe is a type of shepherd's pie and is just as versatile. Add vegetables and herbs of your choice, depending on what you have to hand.

NUTRITIONAL INFORMATION

Calories 496	Sugars 10g
Protein 38g	Fat 17g
Carbohydrate . . .52g	Saturates 9g

10 mins, plus 15 mins cooling time   45 mins

SERVES 4

I N G R E D I E N T S

1 lb 2 oz/500 g minced chicken

1 large onion, finely chopped

2 carrots, finely chopped

2 tbsp plain flour

1 tbsp tomato purée

300 ml/10 fl oz chicken stock

pinch of fresh thyme

1.5 kg/3 lb 5 oz mashed potatoes, creamed with butter and milk and highly seasoned

75 g/2¾ oz grated cheese, such as Cheddar

salt and pepper

cooked peas, to serve

1 Brown the minced chicken, onion and carrots in a non-stick frying pan for 5 minutes, stirring frequently.

2 Sprinkle the chicken with the flour and simmer for a further 2 minutes.

3 Gradually blend in the tomato purée and stock, then simmer for 15 minutes. Season and add the thyme.

4 Transfer the chicken and vegetable mixture to an ovenproof casserole and leave to cool.

5 Spoon the mashed potato over the chicken mixture and sprinkle with cheese. Bake in a preheated oven at 200°C/400°F/Gas Mark 6 for 20 minutes, or until the cheese is bubbling and golden, then serve, straight from the casserole, with the peas.

VARIATION
Instead of plain cheese, you could sprinkle a flavoured cheese over the top. There are a variety of cheeses blended with onion and chives, and these are ideal for melting as a topping. Alternatively, you could use a mixture of cheeses, depending on what you have to hand.

Country Chicken Hotpot

There are many regional versions of hotpot, all using fresh, local ingredients available all year, perfect for traditional one-pot cooking.

NUTRITIONAL INFORMATION

Calories 499   Sugars 6g
Protein . . . . .43g   Fat 17g
Carbohydrate . . .44g   Saturates 8g

10 mins   2 hrs

SERVES 4

I N G R E D I E N T S

4 chicken quarters

6 medium potatoes, cut into
    5 mm/¼ inch slices

2 sprigs thyme

2 sprigs rosemary

2 bay leaves

200 g/7 oz smoked bacon, rinded and diced

1 large onion, finely chopped

2 carrots, sliced

150 ml/5 fl oz stout

2 tbsp melted butter

salt and pepper

1 Remove the skin from the chicken quarters, if desired.

2 Arrange a layer of potato slices in the base of a wide casserole. Season with salt and pepper, then add the thyme, rosemary and bay leaves.

3 Top with the chicken quarters, then sprinkle with the diced bacon, onion, and carrots. Season well and arrange the remaining potato slices on top, overlapping slightly.

4 Pour over the stout, brush the potatoes with the melted butter, and cover with a lid.

5 Bake in a preheated oven, 150°C/300°F/Gas Mark 2, for approximately 2 hours, uncovering the casserole for the last 30 minutes to allow the potatoes to brown. Serve hot, with fresh seasonal vegetables.

VARIATION
This dish is also delicious with stewing lamb, cut into chunks. You can add different vegetables depending on what is in season—try leeks and swede for a slightly sweeter flavour.

Gardener's Chicken

Any combination of small, young vegetables can be roasted with this delicious stuffed chicken, such as courgettes, leeks and onions.

NUTRITIONAL INFORMATION

Calories	674	Sugars	........18g
Protein	........35g	Fat	.........40g
Carbohydrate	...45g	Saturates	......12g

  🕐 10 mins   1 hr 40 mins

SERVES 4

INGREDIENTS

250 g/9 oz parsnips, peeled and chopped

2 small carrots, peeled and chopped

30 g/1 oz fresh breadcrumbs

¼ tsp grated nutmeg

1 tbsp chopped fresh parsley

1.5 kg/3 lb chicken

bunch fresh parsley

½ onion

2 tbsp butter, softened

4 tbsp olive oil

500 g/1 lb 2 oz new potatoes, scrubbed

500 g/1 lb 2 oz baby carrots, washed and trimmed

salt and pepper

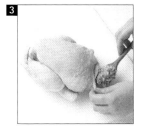

1 To make the stuffing, put the parsnips and carrots into a pan, half cover with water and bring to the boil. Cover the pan and simmer until tender. Drain well, then purée in a blender or food processor. Transfer the purée to a bowl and leave to cool.

2 Mix in the breadcrumbs, nutmeg and parsley and season to taste with salt and pepper.

3 Put the stuffing into the neck end of the chicken and push a little under the skin over the breast meat. Secure the flap of skin with a small metal skewer or cocktail stick.

4 Place the bunch of parsley and onion inside the cavity of the chicken, then place the chicken in a large roasting tin.

5 Spread the butter over the skin and season with salt and pepper, cover with foil and place in a preheated oven, 190°C/375°F/Gas Mark 5, for 30 minutes.

6 Meanwhile, heat the oil in a frying pan, and lightly brown the potatoes.

7 Transfer the potatoes to the roasting tin and add the baby carrots. Baste the chicken and continue to cook for a further hour, basting the chicken and vegetables after 30 minutes. Remove the foil for the last 20 minutes to allow the skin to crisp. Garnish the vegetables with chopped parsley and serve.

Potato & Turkey Pie

Turkey is especially good with fruit, because it has a fairly strong flavour. The walnuts counteract the sweetness of the fruit.

NUTRITIONAL INFORMATION

Calories 790   Sugars 16g
Protein . . . . .28g   Fat 50g
Carbohydrate . . .60g   Saturates 23g

10 mins   50 mins

SERVES 4

INGREDIENTS

300 g/10½ oz waxy potatoes, diced

2 tbsp butter

1 tbsp vegetable oil

300 g/10½ oz lean turkey meat, cubed

1 red onion, halved and sliced

2 tbsp plain flour

300 ml/10 fl oz milk

150 ml/5 fl oz double cream

2 celery sticks, sliced

75 g/2¾ oz dried apricots, chopped

25 g/1 oz walnut pieces

2 tbsp chopped fresh parsley

salt and pepper

225 g/8 oz ready-made shortcrust pastry

beaten egg, for brushing

1 Cook the diced potatoes in a saucepan of boiling water for 10 minutes until tender. Drain and set aside.

2 Meanwhile, heat the butter and oil in a saucepan. Add the turkey and cook for 5 minutes, turning until browned.

3 Add the sliced onion and cook for 2–3 minutes. Stir in the flour and cook for 1 minute. Gradually stir in the milk and the double cream. Bring to the boil, stirring, then reduce the heat until the mixture is simmering.

4 Stir in the celery, apricots, walnut pieces, parsley and potatoes. Season well with salt and pepper. Spoon the potato and turkey mixture into the base of a 1.2-litre/2-pint pie dish.

5 On a lightly floured surface, roll out the pastry until it is 2.5-cm/1-inch larger than the dish. Trim a 2.5-cm/1-inch wide strip from the pastry and place the strip on the dampened rim of the dish. Brush with water and cover with the pastry lid, pressing to seal the edges.

6 Brush the top of the pie with beaten egg and cook in a preheated oven, 200°C/400°F/Gas Mark 6, for 25–30 minutes or until the pastry is cooked and golden brown. Serve at once.

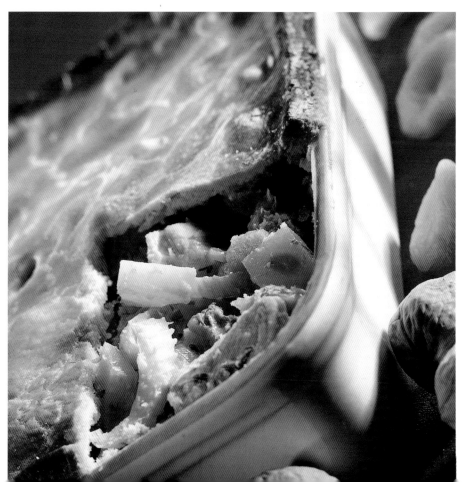

Hotpot Chops

A hotpot is a lamb casserole, made with carrots and onions and with a potato topping. The chops used here are an interesting alternative.

NUTRITIONAL INFORMATION

Calories . . . . . . .250 Sugars 2g
Protein . . . . .27g Fat 12g
Carbohydrate . . . .8g Saturates 5g

10 mins   30 mins

SERVES 4

I N G R E D I E N T S

4 lean, boneless lamb leg steaks, about 125 g/4½ oz each

1 small onion, thinly sliced

1 carrot, thinly sliced

1 potato, thinly sliced

1 tsp olive oil

1 tsp dried rosemary

salt and pepper

fresh rosemary, to garnish

freshly steamed green vegetables, to serve

1 Preheat the oven to 180°C/350°F/Gas Mark 4. Using a sharp knife, trim any excess fat from the lamb steaks.

2 Season both sides of the steaks with salt and pepper and arrange them on a baking tray.

3 Alternate layers of sliced onion, carrot and potato on top of each lamb steak.

4 Brush the tops of the potato lightly with oil, season well with salt and pepper to taste and then sprinkle with a little dried rosemary.

5 Bake the hotpot chops in the oven for 25–30 minutes until the lamb is tender and cooked through.

6 Drain the lamb on absorbent kitchen paper and transfer to a warmed serving plate.

7 Garnish with fresh rosemary and serve accompanied with a selection of green vegetables.

VARIATION

This recipe would work equally well with boneless chicken breasts. Pound the chicken slightly with a meat mallet or covered rolling pin so that the pieces are the same thickness throughout.

Beef & Potato Goulash

In this recipe, the potatoes are actually cooked in the goulash. For a change, you may prefer to substitute small, scrubbed new potatoes.

NUTRITIONAL INFORMATION

Calories 477   Sugars 11g
Protein . . . . .47g   Fat 16g
Carbohydrate . . .39g   Saturates 5g

 15 mins   2¼ hrs

SERVES 4

I N G R E D I E N T S

2 tbsp vegetable oil

1 large onion, sliced

2 garlic cloves, crushed

750 g/1 lb 10 oz lean stewing steak

2 tbsp paprika

400 g/14 oz canned chopped tomatoes

2 tbsp tomato purée

1 large red pepper, cored, deseeded
  and chopped

175 g/6 oz mushrooms, wiped and sliced

600 ml/1 pint beef stock

500 g/1 lb 2 oz potatoes, peeled and cut
  into large chunks

1 tbsp cornflour

salt and pepper

TO GARNISH

4 tbsp low-fat natural yogurt

paprika

chopped fresh parsley

1 Heat the oil in a large saucepan and fry the onion and garlic for 3–4 minutes until softened.

2 Cut the steak into chunks and cook over a high heat for about 3 minutes until browned all over.

3 Add the paprika and stir well. Add the tomatoes, tomato purée, red pepper and mushrooms. Cook the vegetables for 2 minutes, stirring constantly.

4 Pour in the stock. Bring to the boil, then reduce the heat. Cover and simmer for about 1½ hours until the meat is tender.

5 Add the potatoes and cook, covered, for 20–30 minutes until tender.

6 Blend the cornflour with a little water and add to the saucepan, stirring until thickened and blended. Cook for 1 minute then season with salt and pepper. Top with the yogurt, sprinkle over the paprika, garnish with chopped fresh parsley and serve.

Potato, Beef & Peanut Pot

The spicy peanut sauce in this recipe will complement almost any meat; the dish is just as delicious made with chicken or pork.

NUTRITIONAL INFORMATION

Calories 559	Sugars 5g	
Protein 35g	Fat 37g	
Carbohydrate ...24g	Saturates 13g	

 5 mins   1 hr

SERVES 4

INGREDIENTS

1 tbsp vegetable oil

5 tbsp butter

450 g/1 lb lean beef steak, cut into thin strips

1 onion, halved and sliced

2 garlic cloves, crushed

600 g/1 lb 5 oz waxy potatoes, cubed

½ tsp paprika

4 tbsp crunchy peanut butter

600 ml/1 pint beef stock

25 g/1 oz unsalted peanuts

2 tsp light soy sauce

50 g/1¾ oz sugar snap peas

1 red pepper, cut into strips

parsley sprigs, to garnish (optional)

1 Heat the oil and butter in a flameproof casserole dish.

2 Add the beef strips and fry them gently for approximately 3–4 minutes, stirring and turning the meat until it is sealed on all sides.

3 Add the onion and garlic and cook for a further 2 minutes, stirring constantly.

4 Add the potato cubes and cook for 3–4 minutes or until they begin to brown slightly.

5 Stir in the paprika and peanut butter, then gradually blend in the beef stock. Bring the mixture to the boil, stirring frequently.

6 Finally, add the peanuts, soy sauce, sugar snap peas and red pepper.

7 Cover and cook over a low heat for 45 minutes or until the beef is cooked right through.

8 Garnish the dish with parsley sprigs, if desired, and serve.

COOK'S TIP
Serve this dish with plain boiled rice or noodles, if you wish.

Potato Ravioli

In this recipe the 'pasta' dough is made with potatoes instead of flour. The ravioli are filled with bolognese sauce and cooked in a frying pan.

NUTRITIONAL INFORMATION

Calories 559   Sugars 4g
Protein ....17g   Fat 30g
Carbohydrate ...60g   Saturates 11g

5–10 mins   1 hr 10 mins

SERVES 4

I N G R E D I E N T S

FILLING

1 tbsp vegetable oil

125 g/4½ oz minced beef

1 shallot, diced

1 garlic clove, crushed

1 tbsp plain flour

1 tbsp tomato purée

150 ml/5 fl oz beef stock

1 celery stick, chopped

2 tomatoes, peeled and diced

2 tsp chopped fresh basil

salt and pepper

RAVIOLI

450 g/1 lb floury potatoes, diced

3 small egg yolks

3 tbsp olive oil

175 g/6 oz plain flour

5 tbsp butter, for frying

shredded basil leaves, to garnish

1 To make the filling, heat the oil in a pan and fry the beef for 3–4 minutes, breaking it up with a spoon. Add the shallot and garlic and cook for 2–3 minutes until the shallot has softened.

2 Stir in the flour and tomato purée and cook for 1 minute. Stir in the beef stock, celery, tomatoes and chopped fresh basil. Season to taste with salt and pepper.

3 Cook the mixture over a low heat for 20 minutes. Remove from the heat and leave to cool.

4 To make the ravioli, cook the potatoes in a pan of boiling water for 10 minutes until cooked.

5 Mash the potatoes and place them in a mixing bowl. Blend in the egg yolks and oil. Season with salt and pepper, then stir in the flour and mix to form a dough.

6 On a lightly floured surface, divide the dough into 24 pieces and shape into flat rounds. Spoon the filling on to one half of each round and fold the dough over to encase the filling, pressing down to seal the edges.

7 Melt the butter in a frying pan and cook the ravioli in batches for 6–8 minutes, turning once, until golden. Serve hot, garnished with chopped fresh basil leaves.

Veal Italienne

This dish is really superb if made with tender veal. However, if veal is unavailable, use pork or turkey escalopes instead.

NUTRITIONAL INFORMATION

Calories 592   Sugars 5g
Protein . . . . .44g   Fat 23g
Carbohydrate . . .48g   Saturates 9g

🥔 25 mins   🕐 1 hr 20 mins

SERVES 4

I N G R E D I E N T S

5 tbsp butter

1 tbsp olive oil

675 g/1½ lb potatoes, cubed

4 veal escalopes, 175 g/6 oz each

1 onion, cut into 8 wedges

2 garlic cloves, crushed

2 tbsp plain flour

2 tbsp tomato purée

150 ml/5 fl oz red wine

300 ml/10 fl oz chicken stock

8 ripe tomatoes, peeled, seeded and diced

25 g/1 oz stoned black olives, halved

2 tbsp chopped fresh basil

salt and pepper

fresh basil leaves, to garnish

1 Heat the butter and oil in a large frying pan. Add the potato cubes and cook for 5–7 minutes, stirring frequently, until they begin to brown.

2 Remove the potatoes from the pan with a slotted spoon and set aside.

3 Place the veal in the frying pan and cook for 2–3 minutes on each side until sealed. Remove from the pan and set aside.

4 Stir the onion and garlic into the pan and cook for 2–3 minutes.

5 Add the flour and tomato purée and cook for 1 minute, stirring. Gradually blend in the red wine and chicken stock, stirring to make a smooth sauce.

6 Return the potatoes and veal to the pan. Stir in the tomatoes, olives and basil and season to taste with salt and pepper.

7 Transfer to a casserole dish and cook in a preheated oven, 180°C/350°F/Gas Mark 4, for 1 hour or until the potatoes and veal are cooked through. Garnish with basil leaves and serve.

COOK'S TIP

For a quicker cooking time and really tender meat, pound the meat with a meat mallet to flatten it slightly before cooking.

Lamb Hotpot

This classic recipe using lamb cutlets layered between sliced potatoes, kidneys, onions and herbs makes a perfect meal on a cold winter's day.

NUTRITIONAL INFORMATION

Calories ....420 Sugars 2g
Protein ....41g Fat 15g
Carbohydrate ...31g Saturates 8g

🥘 15 mins   🕐 2 hrs

SERVES 4

INGREDIENTS

675 g/1½ lb lean lamb neck cutlets

2 lambs' kidneys

675 g/1½ lb waxy potatoes, scrubbed and thinly sliced

1 large onion, thinly sliced

2 tbsp chopped fresh thyme

150 ml/5 fl oz lamb stock

2 tbsp butter, melted

salt and pepper

fresh thyme sprigs, to garnish

1 Remove any excess fat from the lamb. Skin and core the kidneys and cut them into slices.

2 Arrange a layer of potatoes in the base of a 1.7-litre/3-pint ovenproof baking dish.

3 Arrange the lamb neck cutlets on top of the potatoes and cover with the sliced kidneys, onion and thyme.

4 Pour the lamb stock over the lamb cutlets and season to taste with salt and pepper.

5 Layer the remaining potato slices on top, overlapping to cover the meat and sliced onion completely.

6 Brush the potato slices with the butter, cover the dish and cook in a preheated oven, 180°C/350°F/Gas Mark 4, for 1½ hours.

7 Remove the lid and cook for a further 30 minutes until golden brown on top.

8 Garnish with fresh thyme sprigs and serve hot.

VARIATION

Traditionally, oysters are also included in this tasty hotpot. Add them to the layers along with the kidneys, if wished.

Potato & Lamb Kofta

Kofta is a Greek dish traditionally served threaded onto a skewer.
Here the kofta are served on a plate with a refreshing tzatziki sauce.

NUTRITIONAL INFORMATION

Calories . . . . . . .490 Sugars 5g
Protein . . . . .20g Fat 36g
Carbohydrate . . .24g Saturates 9g

5 mins   45 mins

SERVES 4

INGREDIENTS

450 g/1 lb floury potatoes, diced

2 tbsp butter

225 g/8 oz minced lamb

1 onion, chopped

2 garlic cloves, crushed

½ tsp ground coriander

2 eggs, beaten

vegetable oil, for deep-frying

mint sprigs, to garnish

SAUCE

150 ml/5 fl oz natural yogurt

55 g/2 oz cucumber, finely chopped

1 tbsp chopped mint

1 garlic clove, crushed

1 Cook the diced potatoes in a saucepan of boiling water for 10 minutes until cooked through. Drain, mash until smooth and transfer to a mixing bowl.

2 Melt the butter in a frying pan, add the lamb, onion, garlic and coriander and fry for 15 minutes, stirring.

3 Drain off the liquid from the pan, then stir the meat mixture into the mashed potatoes. Stir in the eggs and season to taste.

4 To make the sauce, combine the yogurt, cucumber, mint and garlic in a bowl and set aside.

5 Heat the oil in a large saucepan or a deep fat fryer to 180°C–190°C/350°F–375°F, or until a cube of bread browns in 30 seconds. Drop spoonfuls of the potato mixture into the hot oil and cook in batches for 4–5 minutes or until golden brown.

6 Remove the kofta with a perforated spoon, drain thoroughly on kitchen paper, set aside and keep warm. Garnish with fresh mint sprigs and serve with the sauce.

COOK'S TIP

These kofta can be made with any sort of minced meat, such as turkey, chicken or pork, and flavoured with appropriate fresh herbs, such as sage or coriander.

Spanish Potato Bake

In this variation of a traditional Spanish dish, *huevos* (eggs) are cooked on top of a spicy sausage, tomato and potato mixture.

NUTRITIONAL INFORMATION

Calories	443	Sugars	.........7g
Protein	........21g	Fat	..........25g
Carbohydrate	...36g	Saturates	......8g

 5 mins   35 mins

SERVES 4

INGREDIENTS

675 g/1½ lb waxy potatoes, diced

3 tbsp olive oil

1 onion, halved and sliced

2 garlic cloves, crushed

400 g/14 oz canned plum tomatoes, chopped

75 g/2¾ oz chorizo sausage, sliced

1 green pepper, cut into strips

½ tsp paprika

25 g/1 oz stoned black olives, halved

8 eggs

1 tbsp chopped fresh parsley

salt and pepper

1 Cook the diced potatoes in a saucepan of boiling water for 10 minutes or until softened. Drain and set aside.

2 Heat the olive oil in a large frying pan, add the onion and garlic and fry gently for 2–3 minutes until the onion has softened.

3 Add the tomatoes and cook over a low heat for about 10 minutes until the mixture has reduced slightly.

4 Stir the potatoes into the pan with the chorizo, green pepper, paprika and olives. Cook for 5 minutes, stirring. Transfer to a shallow ovenproof dish.

5 Make 8 small hollows in the top of the mixture and break an egg into each hollow.

6 Cook in a preheated oven, 220°C/425°F/Gas Mark 7, for 5–6 minutes or until the eggs are just cooked. Sprinkle with parsley and serve with crusty bread.

VARIATION

Add a little spice to the dish by incorporating 1 teaspoon chilli powder in step 4, if desired.

Tomato & Sausage Pan-fry

This simple dish is delicious as a main meal. Choose good sausages flavoured with herbs or use flavoured sausages, such as mustard or leek.

NUTRITIONAL INFORMATION

Calories . . . . . . .458 Sugars 11g
Protein . . . . .21g Fat 25g
Carbohydrate . . .34g Saturates 8g

🍴 5 mins   🕐 30 mins

SERVES 4

INGREDIENTS

600 g/1 lb 5 oz potatoes, sliced

1 tbsp vegetable oil

8 flavoured sausages

1 red onion, cut into 8 pieces

1 tbsp tomato purée

150 ml/5 fl oz red wine

150 ml/5 fl oz passata

2 large tomatoes, each cut into 8 pieces

175 g/6 oz broccoli florets, blanched

2 tbsp chopped fresh basil

salt and pepper

shredded fresh basil, to garnish

1 Cook the sliced potatoes in a saucepan of boiling water for 7 minutes. Drain thoroughly and set aside.

2 Meanwhile, heat the oil in a large frying pan. Add the sausages and cook for 5 minutes, turning the sausages frequently to ensure that they are browned on all sides.

3 Add the onion pieces to the pan and continue to cook for a further 5 minutes, stirring the mixture frequently.

4 Stir in the tomato purée, red wine and the passata and mix together well. Add the tomato wedges, broccoli florets and chopped basil to the pan-fry and mix together carefully.

5 Add the parboiled potato slices to the pan. Cook the mixture for about 10 minutes or until the sausages are completely cooked through. Season to taste with salt and pepper.

6 Garnish the pan-fry with fresh shredded basil and serve hot.

COOK'S TIP

Omit the passata from this recipe and use canned plum tomatoes or chopped tomatoes for convenience.

Potato, Beef & Leek Pasties

Filled with potatoes, cubes of beef and leeks, these pasties make a substantial meal. They are also perfect snacks for a picnic or barbecue.

NUTRITIONAL INFORMATION

Calories 419   Sugars 2g
Protein . . . . .18g   Fat 23g
Carbohydrate . . .38g   Saturates 9g

10–15 mins   50 mins

SERVES 4

INGREDIENTS

butter, for greasing

225 g/8 oz waxy potatoes, diced

1 small carrot, diced

225 g/8 oz beef steak, cubed

1 leek, sliced

225 g/8 oz ready-made shortcrust pastry

1 tbsp butter

salt and pepper

1 egg, beaten

1 Lightly grease a baking tray. Mix the diced potatoes, carrots, beef and sliced leek in a large bowl. Season well with salt and pepper.

2 Divide the pastry into four equal portions. On a lightly floured surface, roll out each portion into a 20-cm/ 8-inch round.

3 Spoon the potato mixture on to one half of each round, to within 1 cm/ ½ inch of the edge. Top the potato mixture with the butter, dividing it equally among the rounds. Brush the pastry edge with a little of the beaten egg.

4 Fold the pastry over to encase the filling and crimp the edges together.

5 Transfer the pasties to the prepared baking tray and brush them with the beaten egg.

6 Cook in a preheated oven, 200°C/400°F/Gas Mark 6, for 20 minutes. Reduce the oven temperature to 160°C/325°F/Gas Mark 3 and cook the pasties for a further 30 minutes.

7 Serve the pasties with a crisp salad or onion gravy.

VARIATION

Use other types of meat, such as pork or chicken, in the pasties and add chunks of apple in step 2, if preferred.

Potato & Meat Filo Parcels

These small parcels are perfect for special occasions. Crisp pastry encases a tasty potato and beef filling, cooked in red wine for a delicious flavour.

NUTRITIONAL INFORMATION

Calories 388   Sugars 5g
Protein .... 15g   Fat 12g
Carbohydrate ...53g   Saturates 5g

 10 mins   35 mins

SERVES 4

INGREDIENTS

225 g/8 oz waxy potatoes, diced finely

1 tbsp vegetable oil

125 g/4½ oz minced beef

1 leek, sliced

1 small yellow pepper, finely diced

125 g/4½ oz button mushrooms, sliced

1 tbsp plain flour

1 tbsp tomato purée

6 tbsp red wine

6 tbsp beef stock

1 tbsp chopped fresh rosemary

225 g/8 oz filo pastry, thawed
    if frozen

2 tbsp butter, melted

salt and pepper

1 Cook the diced potatoes in a saucepan of boiling water for 5 minutes. Drain and set aside.

2 Meanwhile, heat the oil in a saucepan and fry the minced beef, leek, yellow pepper and mushrooms over a low heat for 5 minutes.

3 Stir in the flour and tomato purée and cook for 1 minute. Gradually add the red wine and beef stock, stirring to thicken. Add the chopped rosemary, season to taste with salt and pepper and leave to cool slightly.

4 Lay 4 sheets of filo pastry on a work surface or board. Brush each sheet with butter and lay a second layer of filo on top. Trim the sheets to make four 20- cm/8-inch squares.

5 Brush the edges of the pastry with a little butter. Spoon a quarter of the beef mixture into the centre of each square. Bring up the corners and the sides of the squares to form a parcel, scrunching the edges together. Make sure that the parcels are well sealed by pressing the pastry together, otherwise the filling will leak.

6 Place the parcels on a baking tray and brush with butter. Bake in a preheated oven, 180°C/350°F/Gas Mark 4, for 20 minutes. Serve hot.

Carrot-topped Beef Pie

This is a variation of an old favourite, where a creamy mashed potato and carrot topping is piled thickly on to a delicious beef pie filling.

NUTRITIONAL INFORMATION

Calories ....352 Sugars 6g
Protein ....28g Fat 11g
Carbohydrate ...38g Saturates 6g

 10 mins   🕐 1 hr 15 mins

SERVES 4

I N G R E D I E N T S

450 g/1 lb lean minced beef

1 onion, chopped

1 garlic clove, crushed

1 tbsp plain flour

300 ml/10 fl oz beef stock

2 tbsp tomato purée

1 celery stick, chopped

3 tbsp chopped fresh parsley

1 tbsp Worcestershire sauce

675 g/1½ lb floury potatoes, diced

2 large carrots, diced

2 tbsp butter

3 tbsp skimmed milk

salt and pepper

1 Dry-fry the beef in a large pan set over a high heat for 3–4 minutes or until sealed. Add the onion and garlic and cook for a further 5 minutes, stirring.

2 Add the flour and cook for 1 minute. Gradually blend in the beef stock and tomato purée. Stir in the celery, 1 tablespoon of the parsley and the Worcestershire sauce. Season to taste.

3 Bring the mixture to the boil, then reduce the heat and simmer for

20–25 minutes. Spoon the beef mixture into a 1.2-litre/2-pint pie dish.

4 Meanwhile, cook the potatoes and carrots in a saucepan of boiling water for 10 minutes. Drain thoroughly and mash them together.

5 Stir the butter, milk and the remaining parsley into the potato and

carrot mixture and season with salt and pepper to taste. Spoon the potato on top of the beef mixture to cover it completely; alternatively, pipe the potato over the top with a piping bag.

6 Cook the carrot-topped beef pie in a preheated oven, 190°C/375°F/Gas Mark 5, for 45 minutes or until cooked through. Serve piping hot.

Potato, Beef & Kidney Pie

Steak and kidneys have always been a popular pie filling; this version is very good because it is cooked in a beer sauce with chunks of potato.

NUTRITIONAL INFORMATION

Calories 533   Sugars 4g
Protein ....36g   Fat 26g
Carbohydrate ...39g   Saturates 6g

10 mins   1 hr 35 mins

SERVES 4

I N G R E D I E N T S

225 g/8 oz waxy potatoes, cubed

2 tbsp butter

450 g/1 lb lean steak, cubed

150 g/5½ oz ox kidney, cored and chopped

12 shallots

1 tbsp plain flour

150 ml/5 fl oz beef stock

150 ml/5 fl oz stout

225 g/8 oz ready-made puff pastry

1 egg, beaten

salt and pepper

1 Cook the cubed potatoes in a saucepan of boiling water for 10 minutes. Drain thoroughly.

2 Meanwhile, melt the butter in a saucepan and add the steak cubes and the kidney. Cook for 5 minutes, stirring until the meat is sealed on all sides.

3 Add the shallots and cook for a further 3–4 minutes. Stir in the flour and cook for 1 minute. Gradually stir in the beef stock and stout and bring to the boil, stirring constantly.

4 Stir the potatoes into the meat mixture and season with salt and

pepper. Reduce the heat until the mixture is simmering. Cover the saucepan and cook for 1 hour, stirring occasionally.

5 Spoon the beef mixture into the base of a pie dish. Roll the pastry on a lightly floured surface until it is 1 cm/½ inch larger than the top of the dish.

6 Cut a strip of pastry long enough and wide enough to fit around the edge of the dish. Brush the edge of the dish with

beaten egg and press the pastry strip around the edge. Brush with egg and place the pastry lid on top. Crimp to seal the edge and brush with beaten egg.

7 Cook in a preheated oven, 230°C/450°F/Gas Mark 8, for 20–25 minutes or until the pastry has risen and is golden. Serve while it is hot, straight from the dish.

Raised Pork & Apple Pie

The pastry used in this recipe requires fairly speedy working because it is moulded into the tin while it is warm and pliable.

NUTRITIONAL INFORMATION

Calories	735	Sugars	.........9g
Protein	........25g	Fat	.........32g
Carbohydrate	...93g	Saturates	......14g

20 mins, plus 2 hrs chilling time

2 hrs 35 mins

SERVES 8

INGREDIENTS

FILLING

900 g/2 lb waxy potatoes, sliced

2 tbsp butter

2 tbsp vegetable oil

450 g/1 lb lean pork, cubed

2 onions, sliced

4 garlic cloves, crushed

4 tbsp tomato purée

600 ml/1 pint stock

2 tbsp chopped fresh sage

2 dessert apples, peeled and sliced

salt and pepper

PASTRY

675 g/1½ lb plain flour

pinch of salt

4 tbsp butter

125 g/4½ oz lard

300 m/10 fl oz water

1 egg, beaten

1 tsp gelatine

1 Cook the potatoes in boiling water for 10 minutes. Drain and set aside. Heat the butter and oil in a flameproof casserole dish and fry the pork until browned, turning. Add the onion and garlic and cook for 5 minutes. Stir in the rest of the filling ingredients, except for the potatoes and the apples. Season to taste. Reduce the heat, cover and simmer for 1½ hours. Drain the stock from the casserole dish and reserve. Leave the pork to cool.

2 To make the pastry, sieve the flour into a bowl. Add the salt and make a well in the centre. Melt the butter and lard in a pan with the water, then bring to the boil. Pour into the flour and mix to form a dough. Turn on to a floured surface and knead until smooth. Reserve a quarter of the dough and use the rest to line the base and sides of a large pie tin or deep 20-cm/8-inch loose-bottomed cake tin.

3 Layer the pork, potatoes and apples in the base. Roll out the reserved pastry to make a lid. Dampen the edges and place the lid on top, sealing well. Brush with egg and make a hole in the top. Cook in a preheated oven, 200°C/400°F/Gas Mark 6, for 30 minutes, then at 160°C/325°F/Gas Mark 3 for 45 minutes. Dissolve the gelatine in the reserved stock and pour into the hole in the lid as the pie cools. Serve well chilled with salad.

Potato, Sausage & Onion Pie

This is a delicious supper dish for all of the family. Use good-quality herb sausages for a really tasty pie.

NUTRITIONAL INFORMATION

Calories 399   Sugars 6g
Protein . . . . .14g   Fat 22g
Carbohydrate . . .39g   Saturates 11g

  5–10 mins   40 mins

SERVES 4

INGREDIENTS

2 large waxy potatoes, unpeeled and sliced

2 tbsp butter

4 thick pork and herb sausages

1 leek, sliced

2 garlic cloves, crushed

150 ml/5 fl oz vegetable stock

150 ml/5 fl oz dry cider or apple juice

2 tbsp chopped fresh sage

2 tbsp cornflour

4 tbsp water

75 g/2¾ oz mature cheese, grated

salt and pepper

1 Cook the sliced potatoes in a saucepan of boiling water for 10 minutes. Drain and set aside.

2 Meanwhile, melt the butter in a frying pan and cook the sausages for 8–10 minutes, turning them frequently so that they brown on all sides. Remove the sausages from the pan and cut them into thick slices.

3 Add the leek, garlic and sausage slices to the pan and cook for 2–3 minutes.

4 Add the vegetable stock, cider or apple juice and sage. Season with salt and pepper to taste.

5 Blend the cornflour with the water. Stir it into the pan and bring to the boil, stirring until the sauce is thick and clear. Spoon the mixture into the base of a deep pie dish.

6 Layer the potato slices on top of the sausage mixture to cover it completely. Season with salt and pepper and sprinkle the grated cheese over the top.

7 Cook in a preheated oven, 190°C/375°F/Gas Mark 5, for 25–30 minutes or until the potatoes are cooked and the cheese is golden brown. Serve hot.

Potato & Broccoli Pie

The sauce for this pie is flavoured with rich dolcelatte cheese and walnuts, which are delicious with broccoli.

NUTRITIONAL INFORMATION

Calories	.616	Sugars	.8g
Protein	.22g	Fat	.37g
Carbohydrate	.53g	Saturates	.10g

 5–10 mins   45 mins

SERVES 4

INGREDIENTS

450 g/1 lb waxy potatoes, cut into chunks

2 tbsp butter

1 tbsp vegetable oil

175 g/6 oz lean pork, cubed

1 red onion, cut into 8 pieces

2½ tbsp plain flour

150 ml/5 fl oz vegetable stock

150 ml/5 fl oz milk

75 g/2¾ oz dolcelatte, crumbled

175 g/6 oz broccoli florets

25 g/1 oz walnuts

225 g/8 oz ready-made puff pastry

milk, for glazing

salt and pepper

1 Cook the potato chunks in a saucepan of boiling water for 5 minutes. Drain and set aside.

2 Meanwhile, heat the butter and oil in a heavy-based pan. Add the pork cubes and cook for 5 minutes, turning until browned.

3 Add the onion and cook for a further 2 minutes. Stir in the flour and cook for 1 minute, then gradually stir in the vegetable stock and milk. Bring to the boil, stirring constantly.

4 Add the cheese, broccoli, potatoes and walnuts to the pan and simmer for 5 minutes. Season with salt and pepper, then spoon the mixture into a pie dish.

5 On a floured surface, roll out the pastry until 2.5 cm/1 inch larger than the dish. Cut a 2.5-cm/1-inch wide strip from the pastry. Dampen the edge of the dish and place the pastry strip around it. Brush with milk and put the pastry lid on top.

6 Seal and crimp the edges and make 2 small slits in the centre of the lid. Brush with milk and then cook in a preheated oven, 200°C/400°F/Gas Mark 6, for 25 minutes or until the pastry has risen and is golden.

COOK'S TIP

Use a hard cheese such as mature Cheddar instead of the dolcelatte, if you prefer.

Potato & Ham Pie

This pie contains chunks of pineapple – a classic accompaniment to ham – with potatoes and onion in mustard sauce, and a cheese-flavoured pastry.

NUTRITIONAL INFORMATION

Calories .... .887   Sugars .... .10g
Protein .... .31g   Fat .... .57g
Carbohydrate ...68g   Saturates ..... .34g

 10 mins   55 mins

SERVES 12

INGREDIENTS

225 g/8 oz waxy potatoes, cubed

2 tbsp butter

8 shallots, halved

225 g/8 oz smoked ham, cubed

2½ tbsp plain flour

300 ml/10 fl oz milk

2 tbsp wholegrain mustard

50 g/1¾ oz pineapple, cubed

PASTRY

225 g/8 oz plain flour

½ tsp dry mustard

pinch of salt

pinch of cayenne pepper

150 g/5½ oz butter

125 g/4½ oz mature cheese, grated

2 egg yolks, plus extra for brushing

4–6 tsp cold water

1 Cook the potato cubes in a saucepan of boiling water for 10 minutes. Drain and set aside.

2 Meanwhile, melt the butter in a saucepan, add the shallots and fry gently for 3–4 minutes until they begin to colour.

3 Add the ham and cook for 2–3 minutes. Stir in the flour and cook for 1 minute. Gradually stir in the milk. Add the mustard and pineapple and bring to the boil, stirring. Season well with salt and pepper and add the potatoes.

4 Sieve the flour for the pastry into a bowl with the mustard, salt and cayenne. Rub the butter into the mixture until it resembles breadcrumbs. Add the cheese and mix to form a dough with the egg yolks and water.

5 On a floured surface, roll out half of the pastry and line a shallow pie dish.

6 Spoon the filling into the pie dish. Brush the edges of the pastry carefully with water.

7 Roll out the remaining pastry and press it on top of the pie, sealing the edges. Decorate the top with the pastry trimmings. Brush the pie with egg yolk and cook in a preheated oven, 190°C/375°F/Gas Mark 5, for 40–45 minutes or until the pastry is cooked and golden.

Potatoes Cooked with Meat

Khormas almost always contain yogurt and therefore have lovely, smooth sauces. Chapatis or fried rice make a good accompaniment.

NUTRITIONAL INFORMATION

Calories 737   Sugars 7g
Protein ....27g   Fat 61g
Carbohydrate ...21g   Saturates 16g

5 mins   1 hr 15 mins

SERVES 6

I N G R E D I E N T S

3 onions

675 g/1½ lb potatoes

300 ml/10 fl oz vegetable oil

1 kg/2 lb 4 oz leg of lamb, cubed

2 tsp garam masala

1½ tsp finely chopped fresh root ginger

1½ tsp crushed fresh garlic

1 tsp chilli powder

3 black peppercorns

3 green cardamoms

1 tsp black cumin seeds

2 cinnamon sticks

1 tsp paprika

1½ tsp salt

150 ml/5 fl oz natural yogurt

600 ml/1 pint water

TO GARNISH

2 green chillies, chopped

fresh coriander leaves, chopped

1 Peel and slice the onions and set aside. Peel and cut each potato into 6 equal-sized pieces.

2 Heat the oil in a saucepan and fry the sliced onions until golden brown. Remove the onions from the pan and set aside.

3 Add the meat to the saucepan with 1 teaspoon of the garam masala and stir-fry for 5–7 minutes over a low heat.

4 Add the onions to the pan, remove from the heat, and then set aside.

5 Meanwhile in a small bowl, mix together the ginger, garlic, chilli powder, peppercorns, cardamoms, cumin seeds, cinnamon sticks, paprika and salt. Add the yogurt and mix well.

6 Return the pan to the heat and gradually add the spice and yogurt mixture to the meat and onions and stir-fry for 7–10 minutes. Add the water, lower the heat and cook, covered, for about 40 minutes, stirring the mixture occasionally.

7 Add the potatoes to the pan and cook, covered, for a further 15 minutes, gently stirring the mixture occasionally. Garnish with green chillies and fresh coriander leaves, and serve at once.

Strained Dhaal with Meatballs

This is a dhaal with a difference. After cooking it, add meatballs and a few fried potato wafers. Serve with fried or plain boiled rice and poppadoms.

NUTRITIONAL INFORMATION

Calories ....530 Sugars 1g
Protein ....9g Fat 44g
Carbohydrate ...25g Saturates 5g

 5 mins   40 mins

SERVES 6

I N G R E D I E N T S

200 g/7 oz masoor dhaal

850 ml/1½ pints water

1 tsp crushed fresh root ginger

1 tsp crushed fresh garlic

½ tsp turmeric

1½ tsp chilli powder

1½ tsp salt

3 tbsp lemon juice

450 g/1 lb canned meatballs

TO GARNISH

3 green chillies, finely chopped

fresh coriander leaves, chopped

BAGHAAR

150 ml/5 fl oz vegetable oil

3 garlic cloves

4 dried red chillies

1 tsp white cumin seeds

FRIED POTATOES

pinch of salt

2 medium potatoes, thinly sliced

300 ml/10 fl oz vegetable oil

1 Rinse the lentils, and pick through them to remove any stones.

2 Place the lentils in a saucepan and cover with 600 ml/1 pint of the water. Add the ginger, garlic, turmeric and chilli powder and boil until the lentils are soft and mushy. Add the salt, stirring.

3 Mash the lentils, then push them through a sieve, reserving the liquid. Add the lemon juice to the strained liquid.

4 Stir the rest of the water into the strained liquid and bring to the boil over a low heat. Drop the meatballs gently into the lentil mixture. Set aside.

5 Prepare the baghaar. Heat the oil in a pan. Add the garlic, dried red chillies and white cumin seeds and fry for 2 minutes. Pour the baghaar over the lentil mixture, stirring to mix.

6 For the potato fries, rub the salt over the potato slices. Heat the oil in a frying pan and fry the potatoes, turning, until crisp. Garnish the meatballs with the fried potatoes, chillies and coriander.

Coconut Beef Stir-fry

This is a truly aromatic dish, blending the heat of red curry paste with the aroma and flavour of the lime leaves and coconut.

NUTRITIONAL INFORMATION

Calories	322	Sugars	.........9g
Protein	........18g	Fat	..........18g
Carbohydrate	...24g	Saturates	.......6g

 10 mins   25 mins

SERVES 4

INGREDIENTS

2 tbsp vegetable oil

2 cloves garlic

1 onion

350 g/12 oz rump steak

350 g/12 oz sweet potatoes

2 tbsp red curry paste

300 ml/10 fl oz coconut milk

3 lime leaves

cooked jasmine rice, to serve

1 Heat the vegetable oil in a large preheated wok or large heavy-based frying pan.

2 Peel the garlic cloves and crush them in a pestle and mortar. Thinly slice the onions.

3 Using a sharp knife, thinly slice the beef. Add the beef to the wok and stir-fry for about 2 minutes or until sealed on all sides.

4 Add the garlic and the onion to the wok and stir-fry for a further 2 minutes.

5 Using a sharp knife, peel and dice the sweet potato.

6 Add the sweet potato to the wok with the red curry paste, coconut milk and lime leaves and bring to a rapid boil. Reduce the heat, cover and leave to simmer for about 15 minutes or until the potatoes are tender.

7 Remove and discard the lime leaves and transfer the stir-fry to warm serving bowls. Serve hot with cooked jasmine rice.

VARIATION

If you cannot obtain lime leaves, use grated lime rind instead.

Curried Stir-fried Lamb

This dish is very filling, and only requires a simple vegetable accompaniment or bread.

NUTRITIONAL INFORMATION

Calories ......375 Sugars 6g
Protein ....26g Fat 19g
Carbohydrate ...27g Saturates 6g

 10 mins ⏱ 1 hour

SERVES 4

INGREDIENTS

450 g/1 lb potatoes, diced

450 g/1 lb lean lamb, cubed

2 tbsp medium-hot curry paste

3 tbsp sunflower oil

1 onion, sliced

1 aubergine, diced

2 cloves garlic, crushed

1 tbsp grated fresh root ginger

150 ml/5 fl oz lamb or beef stock

salt

2 tbsp chopped fresh coriander, to garnish

1 Bring a large saucepan of lightly salted water to the boil. Add the potatoes and cook for 10 minutes. Remove the potatoes from the saucepan with a slotted spoon and drain thoroughly.

COOK'S TIP

The wok is an ancient Chinese invention, the name coming from the Cantonese, meaning a 'cooking vessel'.

2 Meanwhile, place the lamb cubes in a large mixing bowl. Add the curry paste and mix well until the lamb is evenly coated in the paste.

3 Heat the sunflower oil in a large preheated wok.

4 Add the onion, aubergine, garlic and ginger to the wok and stir-fry for about 5 minutes.

5 Add the lamb to the wok and stir-fry for a further 5 minutes.

6 Add the stock and cooked potatoes to the wok, bring to the boil and leave to simmer for 30 minutes, or until the lamb is tender and cooked through.

7 Transfer the stir-fry to warm serving dishes and scatter with chopped fresh coriander. Serve immediately.

Bread & Desserts

The potato adds an interesting flavour and texture to loaves and cakes. This section includes a range of unusual recipes, and also shows the qualities of the sweet potato in

combination with fruit and spices, such as the Fruity Potato Cake, which is ideal for any special occasion. There is also a tempting plaited loaf and some smaller treats, such as Potato Muffins and the delicately spiced Potato and Nutmeg Scones. To finish, the Indian Sweet Potato Dessert, which includes protein-rich almonds, will provide a satisfying and nutritious end to any meal.

Cheese & Potato Plait

This bread has a delicious cheese and garlic flavour and is best eaten straight from the oven, as soon as it is the right temperature.

NUTRITIONAL INFORMATION

Calories 387   Sugars 1g
Protein . . . . .13g   Fat 8g
Carbohydrate . . .70g   Saturates 4g

 30 mins, plus 2 hrs rising time   55 mins

SERVES 8

I N G R E D I E N T S

175 g/6 oz floury potatoes, diced

2 x 7 g sachets easy-blend dried yeast

675 g/1½ lb white bread flour

450 ml/16 fl oz vegetable stock

2 garlic cloves, crushed

2 tbsp chopped fresh rosemary

125 g/4½ oz grated Gruyère cheese

1 tbsp vegetable oil

1 tbsp salt

1 Lightly grease and flour a baking tray. Cook the potatoes in a pan of boiling water for 10 minutes, or until soft. Drain and mash.

2 Transfer the mashed potatoes to a large mixing bowl, stir in the yeast, flour and stock and mix to form a smooth dough. Add the garlic, rosemary and 75 g/2¾ oz of the cheese and knead the dough for 5 minutes. Make a hollow in the dough, pour in the oil and knead the dough again.

3 Cover the dough and leave it to rise in a warm place for 1½ hours, or until doubled in size.

4 Knead the dough again and divide it into 3 equal portions. Roll each portion into a sausage shape about 35 cm/14 inches long.

5 Press one end of each of the sausage shapes firmly together, then carefully plait the dough, without breaking it, and fold the remaining ends under, sealing them firmly.

6 Place the plait on the baking tray, cover and leave to rise for 30 minutes.

7 Sprinkle the remaining cheese over the top of the plait and cook in a preheated oven, 190°C/375°F/Gas Mark 5, for 40 minutes, or until the base of the loaf sounds hollow when tapped. Serve while it is warm.

Sweet Potato Bread

This is a great-tasting loaf, coloured light orange by the sweet potato. Added sweetness from the honey is offset by the tangy orange rind.

NUTRITIONAL INFORMATION

Calories 267	Sugars 7g	
Protein 4g	Fat 9g	
Carbohydrate ...45g	Saturates 4g	

20 mins, plus 1 hr 10 mins rising time

1 hr 10 mins

SERVES 8

INGREDIENTS

225 g/8 oz sweet potatoes, diced

150 ml/5 fl oz tepid water

2 tbsp clear honey

2 tbsp vegetable oil

3 tbsp orange juice

75 g/2¾ oz semolina

225 g/8 oz white bread flour

1 sachet easy blend dried yeast

1 tsp ground cinnamon

grated rind of 1 orange

5 tbsp butter

1 Lightly grease a 675 g/1½ lb loaf tin. Cook the sweet potatoes in a saucepan of boiling water for about 10 minutes, or until soft. Drain well and mash until smooth.

2 Meanwhile, mix the water, honey, oil, and orange juice together in a large mixing bowl.

3 Add the mashed sweet potatoes, semolina, three-quarters of the flour, the yeast, ground cinnamon and grated orange rind and mix thoroughly to form a dough. Leave to stand for about 10 minutes.

4 Cut the butter into small pieces and knead it into the dough with the remaining flour. Knead for about 5 minutes, until the dough is smooth.

5 Place the dough in the prepared loaf tin. Cover and leave in a warm place to rise for 1 hour, or until the dough has doubled in size.

6 Cook the loaf in a preheated oven, 190°C/375°F/Gas Mark 5, for 45–60 minutes, or until the base sounds hollow when tapped. Serve the bread warm, cut into slices.

Potato Muffins

Serve this dish while the cheese is still hot and melted, because cooked cheese turns very rubbery if it is allowed to cool down.

NUTRITIONAL INFORMATION

Calories 100   Sugars 11g
Protein . . . . .3g   Fat 2g
Carbohydrate . . .19g   Saturates 1g

 10 mins   30 mins

SERVES 12

INGREDIENTS

butter, for greasing

85 g/3 oz self-raising flour, plus extra for dusting

175 g/6 oz floury potatoes, diced

2 tbsp soft light brown sugar

1 tsp baking powder

125 g/4½ oz raisins

4 eggs, separated

1 Lightly grease and flour 12 muffin tins. Cook the diced potatoes in a saucepan of boiling water for 10 minutes or until cooked. Drain well and mash until smooth.

2 Transfer the mashed potatoes to a mixing bowl and add the flour, sugar, baking powder, raisins and egg yolks. Stir well to mix thoroughly.

3 In a clean bowl, whisk the egg whites until standing in peaks. Using a metal spoon, gently fold them into the potato mixture until fully incorporated.

4 Divide the mixture among the prepared tins.

5 Cook in a preheated oven, 200°C/400°F/Gas Mark 6, for 10 minutes. Reduce the oven temperature to 160°C/325°F/Gas Mark 3 and cook the muffins for 7–10 minutes or until risen.

6 Remove the muffins from the tins and serve warm.

COOK'S TIP

Instead of spreading the muffins with plain butter, serve them with cinnamon butter made by blending 5 tablespoons butter with a large pinch of ground cinnamon.

Potato & Nutmeg Scones

Making these scones with mashed potato gives them a slightly different texture from traditional scones, but they are just as delicious.

NUTRITIONAL INFORMATION

Calories 135   Sugars 6g
Protein ....3g   Fat 4g
Carbohydrate ...23g   Saturates 2g

5 mins   25 mins

SERVES 8

INGREDIENTS

butter, for greasing

225 g/8 oz floury potatoes, diced

125 g/4½ oz plain flour

1½ tsp baking powder

½ tsp grated nutmeg

50 g/1¾ oz sultanas

1 egg, beaten

3 tbsp double cream

2 tsp soft light brown sugar

1 Line and grease a baking tray. Cook the diced potatoes in a saucepan of boiling water for 10 minutes or until soft. Drain well and mash the potatoes.

2 Transfer the mashed potatoes to a large mixing bowl and stir in the flour, baking powder and nutmeg.

3 Stir in the sultanas, egg and cream and beat the mixture with a spoon until smooth.

4 Shape the mixture into 8 rounds about 2 cm/¾ inch thick and place on the baking tray.

5 Cook in a preheated oven, 200°C/400°F/Gas Mark 6, for about 15 minutes or until the scones have risen and are cooked and golden. Sprinkle the scones with sugar and serve warm spread with butter.

COOK'S TIP

For extra convenience, make a batch of scones in advance and freeze them. Thaw thoroughly and warm in a moderate oven when ready to serve.

Fruity Potato Cake

Sweet potatoes mix beautifully with fruit and brown sugar in this unusual cake. Add a few drops of rum or brandy to the recipe if you like.

NUTRITIONAL INFORMATION

Calories 275   Sugars 44g
Protein ....6g   Fat 5g
Carbohydrate ...55g   Saturates 2g

15 mins   1 hr 30 mins

SERVES 6

INGREDIENTS

675 g/1½ lb sweet potatoes, diced

1 tbsp butter, melted

125 g/4½ oz demerara sugar

3 eggs

3 tbsp skimmed milk

1 tbsp lemon juice

grated rind of 1 lemon

1 tsp caraway seeds

125 g/4½ oz dried fruits, such as apple, pear or mango, chopped

2 tsp baking powder

1 Lightly grease an 18-cm/7-inch square cake tin.

2 Cook the sweet potatoes in boiling water for 10 minutes or until soft. Drain and mash until smooth.

3 Transfer the mashed sweet potatoes to a mixing bowl whilst still hot and add the butter and sugar, mixing together well to dissolve.

4 Beat in the eggs, lemon juice and rind, caraway seeds and chopped dried fruit. Add the baking powder and mix well.

5 Pour the mixture into the prepared cake tin.

6 Cook in a preheated oven, 160°C/ 325°F/Gas Mark 3, for 1–1¼ hours or until cooked through.

7 Remove the cake from the tin and transfer to a wire rack to cool. Cut into thick slices to serve.

COOK'S TIP

This cake is ideal as a special occasion dessert. It can be made in advance and frozen until required. Wrap the cake in clingfilm and freeze. Thaw at room temperature for 24 hours and warm through in a moderate oven before serving.

Sweet Potato Dessert

This unusual milky dessert is very quick and easy to make and can be eaten either hot or cold.

NUTRITIONAL INFORMATION

Calories 234   Sugars 23g
Protein . . . . .5g   Fat 3g
Carbohydrate . . .51g   Saturates 1g

15 mins   20 mins

SERVES 10

I N G R E D I E N T S

1 kg/2 lb 4 oz sweet potatoes

850 ml/1½ pints milk

175 g/6 oz sugar

a few chopped almonds, to decorate

1 Using a sharp knife, peel the sweet potatoes. Rinse them and then cut them into slices.

2 Place the sweet potato slices in a large saucepan. Cover with 600 ml/ 1 pint of the milk and cook over a low heat until the sweet potatoes are soft enough to be mashed.

3 Remove the sweet potatoes from the heat and mash thoroughly until completely smooth.

4 Add the sugar and the remaining milk to the mashed sweet potatoes, and carefully stir to blend together.

5 Return the pan to the heat and simmer the mixture until it starts to thicken (it should reach the consistency of a creamy soup).

6 Transfer the sweet potato dessert to a serving dish.

7 Decorate with the chopped almonds and serve immediately.

COOK'S TIP

Sweet potatoes are longer than ordinary potatoes and have a pinkish or yellowish skin with yellow or white flesh. As their name suggests, they taste slightly sweet.

Index